Minority Rules
"Size is not always an indicator of success"

Uncovering four powerful rules to become a
world-impacting minority

By
Randy Schlichting
Copyright June 2015
All Rights Reserved

Minority Rules

"Every great idea eventually degenerates to a thing called work."

Published by **Randy Schlichting** Publishing
For more info email randyschlichting@gmail.com

Minority Rules

Who am I?

I've had the joy of being able to be with, and learn from, some amazingly gifted men and women: Jim Dolas, Kipper Tabb, Bob Carter, Pat Capuano, Nittin Sardar, Ric Tomlinson, Kevin McClellan, Tom Lutz, Steve Brown, Jay Smith, Andrea Williams, Bob Edmiston, Mark Wells, Dennis Bennett, Barbara Beck, Roger Brown, Randy Lawler, and Randy Pope to name a few. They have influenced my thinking greatly.

Dead people like Dietrich Bonhoeffer, Jonathan Edwards, John Owen, Charles Spurgeon, Martin Luther, John Calvin, Hudson Taylor, and George Mueller have also impacted me. I'm grateful that so many have gone before me who were not afraid to ask questions, set out on adventures and write about it all for the ages. Much of my thinking is really a composite of theirs.

I have been blessed to encourage, through discipleship, men like Scott, Robby, Matt, Martin, Chris, Doug, Roy, Jeff, Luke, Phillip, Emilio, Travis, Hung and others. I have learned much from them and my life has been sharpened, even as I have been used to sharpen theirs.

I have also learned much as I have served at Perimeter church for the last 18 years. We have an amazingly broken and gifted congregation who are trying to learn what it means to be loved by Jesus. Our Godly church leadership has taught me much.

Minority Rules

Most importantly, I have been the joyful recipient of a family: A wife of 34 plus years who has shown me grace and love in a way that can not be put into words and three daughters, who have been used by God to show me the depth of my sin, and the ability of my soul to rest in Christ in order to learn how to love well. Two of my daughters are married to the best sons-in-law to date. The third is a graduate from university and is making an impact for Christ through work and her life. It has been, and is, amazing grace.

The ideas I will express here are ones I have been thinking about for a long time, almost 25 years, and I am now wishing I had expressed them, in written form, earlier. Over the years, I have found that whenever I shared the ideas contained in this book, people would say, "Those are great ideas. You should write a book!" So, finally, I did.

I don't claim to know a lot, but I do believe I have learned something significant. That something calls for me to be unequivocal as I write, and I will. That may make you angry. You may wonder who the heck I think I am to say stuff like I do and you may wonder where in the world I came up with the stuff I am writing. Well I want to be transparent and clearly state the point of view from which I write, so I want to reveal an important principle to you up front. Here it is:

Anyone who writes has a worldview. Something is behind them that helped make them think like they do and write as they write. As Jonathan Edwards, the God gifted 18th century pastor once said, everyone has inclinations or affections that cause them to think, talk and act as they do. I am not sure how many authors fess up to that on the front end or how many authors claim to be purely objective, but I do think that writing that does *not* identify its foundational basis, loses some significance because the author has not started from the bottom line: his beliefs. In other words, I don't think the reader should have to guess what is between the lines in order to get the author's motives.

Every writer has some presuppositions about life, death, why we are here, how we got here and where we are going based on something he or she holds to as basic truth. So as you begin to read this, you should be asking questions about me; questions like, "What's at his core?" and "Where is he coming from?"

Most of my core beliefs are based on what I have read in sixty-six books and letters that were written by men who are no longer alive. They were compiled into a book people call the Bible. These works have impacted me and, in effect, have somewhat changed who I am and what I believe. I say *somewhat* because even though I write in light of what I believe, I often don't *live* in light of what I believe. That is a problem we can discuss at some point because it really is our problem. It is a universal issue. But at the end of the day we aspire to live out our worldview.

So, you will have to decide how much of what I write is helpful to your worldview or even fits into it. Maybe you will have to watch as your worldview wrestles with my worldview. I know I've had to do that over the years as I read what other authors wrote. So, I encourage you to read away and take note as to what fits, what does not, and what could be worth wrestling about.

I am thinking many who read this book will be favorable towards Christianity. For those of you who are not, I want to say this book is for you. You may be helpful to me as you read, reflect and perhaps resonate with what I have to say.

My guess is we Christians have ignored you, caused you to wonder what in the world we are doing or, offended you along by the way we think and act. I am sorry that we have, and I hope that you will be able to see, as you read, that I want us to be more like I think you think our leader is: loving, kind, compassionate and good neighbors. Perhaps after you have read this we can talk. I would especially love to get feedback from you.

Prologue
Power

Kings and countries have gone to war over it. Religions have crusaded to re-gain it. Husbands have divorced wives in an ultimate show of it. Families have been shattered in a struggle over who has the most. Perhaps the driving quest for power is the key motivator behind most of the actions of men and women both individually and collectively.

Secretly or openly, we all want power don't we? Having power, gives us the ability to accomplish things that we want to do. The more power we have, the less likely it is that we will be ruled by others *and* the more likely it is that we can make things change to fit our view of the world.

Power is addictive. If we have some power, we want more power. Everybody desires more power in some area of his or her life. Career, business, politics, weight management, kids, spouse, teachers, finances; you name it. We all want more power over some*one* or some*thing*. Many of us are willing to spend most of our waking hours figuring out how to get it. We think thoughts like, *"If I could get those people to...."* or, *"If he would just listen to me..."* or, *"When I have control, then I will..."* as we dream of getting our way.

The road to power starts with us as babies crying, *"Change my diaper; I'm wet!!"* and continues throughout our natural lives. As we walk, or even run, on the road to power, over time we begin to notice that many others are running with us. At some point in the journey we get the sense that, some, if not most of them, appear to be making better headway than we are. A few of them are actually gaining power *at our expense*. That realization can either lead to frustration and a re-doubling of effort to gain power or, it can lead to a feeling of despondency, withdrawal and surrender.

For some of us, the quest for power progresses to the recruiting of others to band together with us so we can press a collective position. If we are determined enough, we find ourselves forming or joining societies, political parties, communities or some other group that shares our worldview.

As we join groups, it is inevitable that the group we are in challenges, or is challenged, by another group for ideological or practical supremacy. The group who can garner the most power through votes or force becomes the victorious majority. The majority rules and the minority have to live with it.

If you're anything like me, perhaps the addiction to power has gotten the better of you from time to time. I have found that even when I gain some power, it is never enough. To gain more, I have found myself doing and saying things that could be construed as controlling. I resemble an addict longing for the next fix. Win one and lose two, always straining for the ultimate victory but, over time, becoming exhausted from the never-ending battle. It is then that insecurity begins to creep in and I begin to wonder what it is all about. I ask myself, *"Is the pursuit of power worth the cost?"*

When I closely examine my life, the truth is, that most of the time, I am impotent. The things I want to have happen do not happen and the majority of people do not do things the way I think they should. To compound the matter, my life is primarily and inextricably linked to a small group that frequently loses whatever the ideological war of the day is. Neither I, nor my group, seem to have whatever it takes to make an impact or successfully persuade others to see it our way. The majority sees it, and lives it their way.

It took me many years to come to the conclusion that I am part of a marginalized, minority group. I denied it for years even as the evidence mounted. Over time, I capitulated and embraced my minority status. To my surprise, when I did, I found great joy. *Say what?* Yes, I found great joy in it because the realization led me to another path and four rules to live by that are taking me out of the "power struggle" mode of existence. I have discovered I am a minority and minorities must live differently to be healthy. My people are a minority people and I, along with them, must recover what it means to live by the rules of our people: minority rules.

Somewhat paradoxically, I am convinced that my group has been shown a pathway, by those who have gone before us, that will enable us to live lives that produce amazing results. To do that, we need to use the specific

Minority Rules

power that has been given to us in a healthy way *and* we need to look to four essential rules. Mysteriously, I believe, if we will recognize our status and aspire with intentionality to live these four rules; we will transform the world in a way that we never thought possible.

Contents

1	Who is a minority?	13
2	Groupies	23
3	How they see us	33
4	How we got here	53
5	Learning from minorities	63
6	Creating a healthy minority	83
7	Minority rules	89
8	The power of minority rules	105
	Onward afterward	113
	An apologetic	115

Minority Rules

Chapter One
Who is a Minority?

"A dead thing can go with the stream, but only a living thing can go against it."
GK Chesterton *Everlasting Man*

You are either in the majority or in the minority. There are either more people like *you* or more people like *them*. If you find yourself in any given demographic sampling, it is wise to know where you really stand, not where you *think* you stand. Whether the head count will be made by race, age, gender, citizenship, or creed, rarely will there be a tie. Some group is always larger and stronger than some other group.

More importantly, if a vote is held on any given issue in which the same *types* of people vote in the same *way*, your group either has enough votes to prevail or they do not. It is simple math; majority rules and the majority have the power.

All of us have had the experience of being in the majority, and the experience of being in the minority. If your candidate won the last election, you know what I am talking about. If he or she did not win, well, then you *really* know what I am talking about. Whatever the result of the last vote, most of us do not walk around each day saying to ourselves or others *"Look at me! I am a minority"* or, *"Here I am. I am in the majority."* Neither role is intrinsically right, wrong, good or bad. One just has more democratic power than the other. It is simple math;

Minority Rules

you are a minority or a majority, and the majority rules, if there is a vote.

Have you ever thought of your status as part of some demographic group? I can tell you, as a white middle-aged male; I had not given it much thought until the past few years. I never had cause to consider myself anything but the majority until something began to gnaw at me; something that I could not shake and, over time, I began to see some things in a new light.

Now perhaps you are already thinking, "*What am I?*" I can help by saying, "*Both!*" Now that may sound strange. But think about it with me. If you are a woman you are in the minority on the planet. If you are a woman you are a minority in terms of CEO positions in Fortune 500 companies. If you are a woman you are in the majority of all people who teach. If you are a male doctor, you are in the majority of that group. Are you black? You are a minority in America, but not in Nigeria.

You get the idea. We are both; depending on the role or demographic sampling the statisticians choose to take at any given time. Does it matter? Does it really make a difference if you are a minority or a majority? Sometimes it does and sometimes not, but, what always matters is *how you, and those who are like you, live out your status in the context of those who are not like you.*

What matters even more is how you identify the *primary* minority or majority group that you associate yourself with. That key identification will have a massive bearing on how you make decisions because when the pressure is on, you will default to that identity.

I have often said that everyone wants to be in a gang. It is part of being human to belong. We have a need to be accepted in community. So, from the time we are kids on the playground we choose teams. We move on to Boy Scouts, Little League, Sororities, Rotary and AARP. We all want to belong.

To complicate matters further, you may find that from time to time you are a member of two groups that may be in conflict with one another. Both groups may tug on you to give what you have, and who you are, to them. It gets tough when that happens, as peer pressure can be immense. When a point of decision comes at which the two groups you belong to are at odds, you have to choose which affiliation is most important. That can have consequences that are challenging and even life changing. Do you choose gang membership or your family; the "in crowd" at school or your best friend; your co-workers night out at the ball game or religious duties at the local church? Those are hard choices that can shape your near and long term future.

This book is an attempt to encourage us all to see the importance of who we are, how we live and to bring to light the fact that, when we know who we are and, which of our minority or majority affiliations is the most important to us, we can move towards healthiness, making decisions in light of a clear set of values regardless of whether we are in the minority or majority.

Minority Rules

So where do we start? Knowledge of where your group stands in relation to other groups is useful. In other words, knowing if you are in the majority or the minority can be helpful. In many areas of your life you could quickly figure out where you stand. But I have found that in some areas, it is easy to think incorrectly about where I am. As an example, it is easy for me to think I am in a poor minority. I live in an affluent area of America and am surrounded by people who have household incomes in excess of six figures. Big houses and fine cars abound. It is easy for me to get the impression that I am a minority on the wealth index. If I widen the lens a bit, just a bit, to Atlanta, let alone Africa, I find that I really am in the minority; the other minority. I am rich. Most people, in fact the vast majority of people, make less than I do. I am in the minority of rich people.

In what way could I think I am in the majority, when in fact I am a minority? How about the fact that I hold to American ideals of democracy? I often think that our values and views are the majority report in the world and that we are working to correct the thinking of the minority who hold views contrary to "truth and justice" for all. Not true. The majority of the world does not think like America, act like Americans or have the same democratic values that we have. We are a minority.

So, it is useful to examine where and who we are in light of where and who we *think* we are. What is *not* useful is being in a group that collectively thinks and acts like it is the majority when it is the minority. Not only is that foolish, it can actually be harmful to the cause of your group. Until you know the truth of where you stand, and examine your actions to see if they line up with your position, you cannot be freed to make changes that would promote health in your group. Having laid that groundwork, I want to shout out the real point of this book.

This book is about uncovering the reality that Christians are a minority in America but collectively we think and act as if we are the majority to the demise of our movement.

People like to be winners, to be in the majority; Americans most of all. Christians who are Americans love to be winners too. After all, we are part of the American experience. As George C. Scott said in the opening scene of the movie "Patton" *"Americans love a winner and hate a loser!"* From the greatest generation to landing on the moon, to the tearing down of the Berlin wall, we have been winners. Internationally we view ourselves as the leaders of the free world. Within America, on the national, state and local level we want things to go our way too. We want our community to reflect who we are and we want the majority of our neighbors to hold our beliefs, even if they do not look exactly like we do.

In reality, sometimes, "we the people" are divided. Some of us are blue and some of us are red. Some of us are in favor of immigration reform and some of us want to build a wall. Some of us want more religion in schools and some of us want less. When there is disagreement over how things should be handled we do what is American, we politic, debate and vote. It is then that some of us become losers.

All of us have experienced the inability to muster up enough people to agree with us on an issue be it what game to play in the school yard or what restaurant to go to for dinner. When that happens, when we lose a debate but still hold to our views, and come to grips with the fact that we are now the minority, we have a choice: to float downstream like dead men along with the majority or to stay alive and embrace our minority status, keeping concerned and active while avoiding bitterness. It is not helpful to act like we won the vote and that the world will sing to our tune, when in reality the music has changed. If we passionately think we are right, we will continue to seek to persuade, but while we do, we must embrace who and what we are. This book is about Christians embracing their minority status in an authentic and healthy way.

I will not win a Nobel Prize for pointing out that it is very hard to go against the cultural stream we find ourselves moving along in. American culture is powerful and persuasive and we can do little as individuals to change it. Our culture is a mosaic, twisted together by politicians, businessmen, educators and philosophers. It is dramatically complex and it is difficult to understand what drives it or causes it to change. A myriad of 'majority status' groups reign over different aspects of culture; a media group, a technology group, a political group and a socially elite group among others. Minority groups

Minority Rules

abound too but they have been so deeply marinated in American culture that most just float down stream, dead to the possibility of making an impact. In fact, our tendency is to choose to join in with a majority group because the benefits of being in it seem to out weigh the cost of minority status. I believe Christians in the main have done exactly that. This book is a call to Christians to live as a minority within the context of American culture by adopting what I call minority rules.

I love Chesterton's quote *"A dead thing can go with the stream, but only a living thing can go against it"* because it is a vivid word picture. If you are dead, you have no choice but to float with the stream. But, if you are alive, you can swim, even while knowing that the current works against you, the undertow is violent and the rocks are sharp. Those who really are passionate can do no other; swim they must. Sadly, few make headway, because they do not know the rules that will help them not only swim against the current but perhaps even change the course of the stream a bit.

They do not know how to gain true power and they quickly tire, becoming as dead men, telling no tales of victory, floating along, only to wake up further down the stream, a bit wetter for the distance, wondering how they got there and wishing they would have hung on for dear life to a branch or, even better, been able to find a place to climb out. Perhaps then they would have been able to gather with others and dream of a way to use the current against itself to create something beautiful. Fewer will make the attempt. It is easier to float along and, in any case, being countercultural has been tried, usually failing miserably or changing little, at a very great cost. This book is about Christians learning to swim with passion and dreaming enough to create a movement inspired by minority rules that could change the course of the stream and be something beautiful for God.

You may have two questions, or more, about now. *"Are Christians really a minority?"* and *"What are minority rules?"* Some of you will be tempted to turn to the end of the book to find the answers and read the rules, knowing clever authors put the good stuff at the front and back of the book. *"Are there ten, seven or three rules?"* you might ask. *"How can they be applied quickly?"* Well, feel free to look. I am glad you bought the book, even if just to skim it. I admit that I do that with books I buy. I do hope you will stick with me here though and let me build a bit of a foundation so that the rules will make more sense. It is a short work and hopefully worth the read.

One last point before we get started. This is for those of you who hate rules. As often is the case, a word picture is helpful. I love the move "Pirates of the Caribbean". At one critical juncture in the movie we learn about the Pirate Code. Some mistakenly think it is a set of hard and fast rules. Not so. It is really a set of guidelines. I would love for you to view the minority rules as that; they are a set of guidelines. They are a way of looking at the world and life that may enable us who are Christians to live in a healthy way because we *are* the minority. We do not have enough votes to turn the tide in the direction we want, we do not have enough power to claim victory and *we never*

Minority Rules

will. By divine providence Christians are a minority and we need rules to live by in order to be healthy and not bitter, energized and not lethargic. That is what this book is about. It will not take long for me to make my points. I hope that it will be helpful to those of us who recognize our status, embrace it and then begin to think about the beauty of minority rules.

Questions to ponder

1. Can you think of a time when you wanted something and did not get it? What stopped you?

2. Think of areas of life in which you are in the majority and in which you are in the minority. How does it feel different when you think about your minority roles and your majority roles?

3. Can you think of a time you were conflicted between two groups you were a member of? How did you resolve the tension?

4. When you think about rules, what emotions come to mind? How does the example from Pirates of the Caribbean help, if at all?

5. Have you ever considered using "minority" as an adjective to describe Christians in America? What difference do you think it would make for Christians to be recognized as a minority?

Chapter Two
Groupies

"Tradition means giving votes to the most obscure of all classes, our ancestors. It is the democracy of the dead. Tradition refuses to submit to the small and arrogant oligarchy of those who happen to be walking about."
G.K. Chesterton

Over the years I have learned that it does not matter much if you are on the playground or in the work yard. People naturally group together, drawing lines so that some are on the inside and others on the outside. I found out that in the adult world the problems caused by groups being formed are at the heart of every conflict. In the beginning, man and woman were of one tribe, but soon enough division happened that sides were chosen. From that day to this, mankind has "picked teams" and staked out territory. We have done it through geography, language, culture and sports. Once sides have been chosen, we have set about competing for supremacy. To determine that, eventually some type of match is played with a winner declared.

Real and sometimes deadly conflict between groups happens all the time. No matter when you turn the news on, you can always hear about the messy world we live in. The general theme is "they" and "we." Democrats and Republicans, Bosnians and Serbs, Catholics and Protestants, Egyptian Islamist and Egyptian Secularists, Palestinians and Israelis are all at odds. Majorities and minorities continue to be defined and polarization is increasing at an alarming rate. Countries vie for power with other countries and states with other states. Texans might only being half joking when they say, *"What do we really have to do with those in New Jersey?"*

On this planet there are groups with power and those without, those with oil and those without, those with some sense of democracy and those with no sense of it at all, those who influence culture, education and thinking and those who would like to influence them but are unable. Everyone wants to and needs to go to their own corner but they define "their corner" as larger than others want them to define it, so conflict erupts.

To further deepen the divide, communities of people eventually break down into families and families into individuals. The "we" of our parent's generation has given way to the "I" of individualism. As a result we have 6.2 billion distinct groups in the world. I can focus on me and my iPod, my iPhone, my Google home page, my text message enabled phone, my Twitter, my Starbucks, MySpace and create my own world. Was Paul Simon right? Are we rocks and islands? The reality is that people *have* created their own worlds, which, from time to time, intersect, with other people's worlds and something like relationship happens.

The media has recognized this, applauds it and reinforces it. In 2006 Time Magazine, which had over the years chosen powerful leaders as their "Man of the Year," chose you. Yes, you were Time's "Man of the Year." That sounds funny doesn't it? In every prior year, Time had

Minority Rules

chosen some one who was a leader of a community, someone who accomplished something significant and made an impact on an identified group of people. In 2006, Time was effectively saying that what is most important is individualism, what you can do by yourself and for yourself. What you do may have a positive impact on others, but it really is about you.

Religious groups abound. Three large religions and a handful of smaller ones look like the total picture, but scratch beneath the surface and you will find sub groups within every strain of religion. Christianity is no exception. There is little sense of community in the church universal, little sense of shared purpose and minimal sense of shared cause. How many denominations do we have now and how are they working together? Are churches within within their own denomination even working together? If the central truth of Christianity is that Jesus gave His life for His people and He calls us to minister in His name in a temporal place, knowing that heaven is for eternity and this life is like a vapor, how might we be seeing churches, Christians and denominations working as one toward that end? Granted, there are pockets of connectedness in selected churches in a few cities, but in general there is little togetherness among those who claim to believe in the same Lord and to have the same mission. We are religious groupies.

So why all the groups and does it matter? Why can't we all just get along and be the human race? The answer is that we are predisposed to groups, to building walls and to shooting arrows. It is the nature of man and has been since the beginning of time. There will always be groups, some large and powerful and some small and weak. Coca Cola may have wanted to teach the world to sing in perfect harmony, but it is not going to happen. Groups are here to stay.

The questions to explore are, "What group am I first and foremost a member of?" and "How healthy is my group?" I know that I am a member of the Christian group and as I examine it I see some significant unhealthiness that needs to be addressed.

Here is my thesis:

"Christians are a minority group, but we live like the majority to the demise of our movement. We have little impact on our culture, we are marginalized because people know we are a minority group trying to act like the majority and so we miss our true call to follow our leader and make a difference that could have beautiful consequences."

Christians are a minority. I am not sure if that statement shocks you, offends you or makes absolutely no impact on you at all, because you think it is ridiculous, irrelevant, or a such a common fact that you can't believe I am writing a book about it. I am an American, white and male with one wife and three daughters. I have grown up in middle class suburbia and "my people" have always been the majority. When I became a Christian I assumed majority status continued. I was wrong. I think I was mistaken because when I first became a Christian I saw

Minority Rules

Christians acting like they were the majority, holding the belief that America was founded as a Christian nation and believing they influenced what was right in every area of American life. Some might say that even now, Judeo Christian values are the majority report. It is as if we live by the quote from Chesterton. It is as if Christians are saying, "We are still counting the votes of those who have gone before us and with their votes we are a majority."

Those are the same people will also point to polls suggesting that 70% of Americans are Christians. Wishful thinking but reality tells me something different.

Those who really are not Christians have swelled the Christian ranks and consequently there is an illusion of majority. Here are the facts. There are over 300 million Americans. Of those, some 70% say they are Christian. That, by the way, is down from 85% in 1990. If the trend does not change, even the people who label themselves as Christian will be a minority by 2040. But the situation is much closer at hand and much more desperate. Scratching beneath the surface, it is easy to see a degenerated picture of Christianity.

For example, currently about 20% of America's Lutherans, 20% of Episcopalians, 18% of Methodists, and 22% of Presbyterians affirm the basic Protestant tenet that by good works man does not earn his way to heaven. That is startling. That means almost 80% of those surveyed, do not think you can be saved by faith alone through Christ alone. Martin Luther would not only roll over in his grave if he could, but he would rise from the dead to have a say about that. John Knox would slap somebody.

So is the "70% of Americans are Christians" sloppy statistical work? My guess is many statisticians take answers at face value. In other words, if someone says that they are a Christian they are recorded as being a Christian.

Lets scratch a bit more now. Why do you think only 20% of churchgoers believe you are saved by faith alone through Christ alone? Answer: the other 80% have not been taught, or have rejected the presupposition. Part of the responsibility for that lies with the church. In the last 50 years the church at large has lost the nerve to live and preach the gospel in a biblical way. Francis Schaeffer said we would lean, even in the church, toward wanting personal peace and affluence and that is what has happened. As a result the gospel is not preached fully because to preach it fully comes with a counter cultural cost. When it is not preached fully, it has no power. So fewer people know the true gospel.

But there is good news and better statistics. By asking some probing questions to refine the definition of a Christian, George Barna the researcher comes up with this descriptive of a Christian:

"Being born again (conversion), saying their faith is very important in their life today; believing they have a personal responsibility to share their religious beliefs about Christ with non-Christians; believing that Satan exists; believing that eternal salvation is possible only through grace, not works; believing that Jesus Christ lived a sinless life on earth; asserting that the Bible is accurate in all that it teaches; and describing God as the all-knowing, all-powerful, perfect deity who created the universe and still rules it today."

When he asks the question that way, he comes to the conclusion that there are about 20 million American adults who would be classified as Christians. That is less than 8% of the population. We could go a step further and ask how many of that 8% (let's include me in that segment) are actually living out their beliefs say 50% of the time. That is certainly not a majority *and* it is good news to know, as I will explain.

Other researchers have begun to dig around the edges of the "face value" answers and have come up with similar statistics. I might add here, statistics aside; I can use my eyes to see that, as I am driving to church on Sunday morning, the rush hour traffic is not quite what it is on Monday. Church attendance does not tell the whole story, but it is an indicator. If you don't go to Rotary meetings, can we call you a Rotarian? You can see how I might come to the conclusion that Christians are a minority but my point is deeper. We are not just a minority (like 46%) we are a tiny minority that is shrinking.

In the rest of the world the figures would of course be more severe, although in parts of Africa, the ratios might be higher. Collectively I think it can be said that

Minority Rules

Christians are a minority. It would be good for us to own that, to meditate on that, and to have the adjective marinate our souls so that we can start to live as a minority would, thereby dropping the decaying lifestyle we cling to in order to become part of an exhilarating future. Christians are a minority. In the chapters ahead I will describe how we live like the majority and how that is causing the demise of our movement.

Minority Rules

Questions to ponder

1. Mark Twain said there are three kinds of lies: lies, damned lies and statistics. Sometimes statistics can be used to bolster a weak argument. Do you think that has been the case with reports of America as a Christian nation?

2. A recent poll in Great Britain revealed that 70% of Brits do not believe in the virgin birth of Christ. Do you think that is good news for the church to know? How can they use that information?

3. If you somewhat meet the definition above for how a Christian acts and believes, can you share why it is a struggle to live that way?

4. Have you ever considered yourself a "groupie"? What image comes to mind as you reflect on that term?

Minority Rules

Chapter Three
How they see us

"For every complex problem, there is usually a simple answer and it's usually wrong."   H.L. Mencken

It is the call of Christians to transcend barriers between tribes, tongues and nations but we don't. Instead we adopt a groupie mindset and establish our own territory to be defended at any cost. Then, to make matters worse, we look to the world and mimic what they do, all the while *decrying* what they do. Crazy. We live like the majority, adopting majority rules and the majority takes note. Here is how they see us:

We drive similar cars, live in similar houses and entertain in similar ways. We have about the same number of kids and have the same amount of debt. We hope in the same material things, are afraid of the same things and try to get ahead on the road to power in the same ways.

Our lives look remarkably similar to people who are not Christians. In our quest for personal peace and affluence we have co-opted our brains to think we can be just like the world and in doing so we have convinced ourselves that we are the majority because the majority of people who claim to be Christians do the things we do.

If we compare us to the early church, the Christians of the reformation, or the Puritans it becomes evident we are not living in light of what we believe to be true. They were seen as radically different. Now go deeper and look

Minority Rules

to Christ. What did He say and how did He call us to live? I find that reading the text is convicting. We can sugar coat it all we want, but the truth is we do not often live the gospel of Jesus; we live the way of the world and the world sees it.

I think it is good for us to admit that and not transition too quickly by saying, *"Lord forgive us for not living like You want us to and thank You Jesus for paying for our sin of living like the world. Amen."* I suggest we just say we are not living well and leave it at that for a while.

Let the weight of that sin bear down without seeking relief too quickly. When we seek relief too quickly, as John Owen the 17th century pastor and theologian said, we are applying the bandage ourselves. We need the Spirit to do the work. He is the one who brings true conviction and He is the only one who can really change us. Far too often we want a "wiping away" for our sin when what we need is a "grieving over" our sin.

The challenge is that we, the people of the church, are eaten up with running after what others run after in the way they run after it. While we live in the material world, we dabble in the spiritual and we fail to steward what we have been given. We consistently look to technology as our god, in our minds we plan to isolate at retirement, hoarding what we have accumulated all the while shaking a fist at the world and telling them what we are against. And you know what? They take note. They see us for who we are and they can describe us better than we can describe ourselves.

As I walk through some descriptions that reveal how the world sees us, can I encourage you, if you are a Christian, to take a deep breath and at least pretend for a moment that I am right? If we can rest in our collective sin, it will be a good first step to healing and wholeness for us as a community. Let's start with materialism.

They see us as materialists

We are a materially obsessed group. We love the material world from bodies to machines. We are focused on getting more of the material word and hanging on to as much of the material body as we can. We have more square feet per person of living area then ever in history, we have more access to transportation than ever before, and we have an incredible focus on obtaining and using the newest leisure toy invented by man. Those are all signs of a materialistic culture. Additionally we have personally adopted the mindset of leveraged buyout living. Buy on borrowed money and over time you will grow your income and payback with cheaper dollars. Growth will make you rich and eliminate the debt. The only problem is that the temptation to borrow more and more is too great and dollars in real terms do not always get cheaper, hence the current economic crisis. But the hunger for the next material fix burns in our stomachs and we borrow and buy regardless of the consequences. How did this mindset develop?

I think it finds its roots in man's desire to be independent and eternal. Both of those attributes are what theologians call incommunicable. God is independent and eternal. He had no beginning and will have no end. He does not need anyone and he does not share that facet of his being with us. We, on the other hand, are dependent on Him and we had a beginning; the moment He created us in His image.

God and we cannot *both* be independent, but that is what we want. We think if we get enough stuff and enough knowledge, we will not be dependent. So we are obsessed with innovation. The spark that lit that roaring obsession can be found in the Enlightenment leading to the Industrial Revolution.

No doubt, the Industrial Revolution was a help to the well being of society. I do like a cool house in the summer. But it brought with it a deeper and darker side of desire within man to possess the next thing so he could have more: more leisure, more power, and more influence. It did not uncork the demon but it fed it so richly that the addiction has overwhelmed generations from then until now. Ever since, we have been innovating, hoping for the final innovation of eternal life with perfect health and inexhaustible resources. That would mean Heaven on earth.

Adding fuel to the fire, the people, who were elected to govern by "we the people", set the culture for borrow and spend materialism. Why save when you can borrow and spend? As of this writing the national debt is over nineteen trillion dollars and growing. Why? The government (us) wanted to buy things to satisfy people and we (it) did not have the cash on hand for them.

Minority Rules

We who are Christians know the scriptures about the debtor being a slave to the lender. We just don't care. Because we enter into debt to get the material things we want, we are in bondage.

To make matters worse, we do not save well. The Commerce Department's figures on Americans' personal savings rate, the amount of disposable income left after taxes and spending each month, tells the story. We are spending what we make and then some. Since dipping to a low of -1% in 2006, in recent year, people have been saving 2% of their income, but there is no reason to believe this will improve further, given historical trends.

The fact that we spend more than we make is just half of the problem. The other half is what we do *not* spend our money on.

As Christians, how much do we spend on the cause of Christ? How much of our time, attention and resources are spent on the cause as opposed to our own individual causes? Most surveys show that fewer than 3% of Christians even tithe; so the reality is: "not much."

A healthy minority on the other hand spends most waking hours and most of its available dollars on the cause. I had lunch one day with five younger men who are in ministry and we got into a discussion about working hard and material gain. Several of the men had some great thinking about wealth viz a viz Christianity. They understood that the love of money is a root of evil and they understood that it does not mean you are a better

Minority Rules

Christian if you have money. They had a moderate approach to gaining wealth, setting aside for the future and keeping out of debt.

As I listened I thought it was good and at the same time I was grieved. So I asked, "Why do you think Catholics ask people like us (people who are in ministry) (ie) priests to take a vow of poverty?" Silence. Now I am not Catholic and I do not agree with all catholic doctrine and dogma. However, using a question like that can help us clear our thinking up a bit. Questions like, "Why is it that not all Christians have great wealth?" should be pondered with observations and better questions. Example: "Do you think more of the wealth in the world is in the hands of Christians or non Christians?" If God values material wealth, it seems He would decree His people to have much of it. Apparently He does not. So does He want His people to live in poverty? Is that the right question? Are most of the poor in the world Christians?

I think better thinking might say that the kingdom has different values. What is valuable in the kingdom is not what is valuable to the world. Does that make sense? Here is a quick clarifying picture. If I go to England, I can take US dollars with me, but they have no value there. I need Sterling. I need to convert what I do have to a currency that is usable in the United Kingdom.

So what is valuable in the kingdom of God? That is what God wants to give us; what is valuable. If we have anything else, we need to see if we can exchange it, release it or surrender it for what is valuable in the kingdom. In fact we may need to release it before we can hold on to what is valuable.

So dollars can be converted to giving. Time can be released to serving. Talking can be surrendered for listening. Gifts we have can be converted into what is useful in the kingdom. We do not accept a vow of material poverty, but we do accept a life that calls us to seek first what is valuable in the kingdom.

In one of the funniest skits I have ever seen, comedian Bob Newhart plays a counselor who has a patient come to see him for help. "The charge is $5 for five minutes," he states. The person, though puzzled, gives him the money and begins to explain her issues and concerns including some dramatic fears. Newhart says, "Stop it!" The patient asks, "Stop what?" Newhart replies, "Stop having those thoughts, stop worrying, and stop it!" The patient says she cannot just stop and Newhart says, "Yes, yes you can. Stop it!"

I sometimes wonder if Jesus might say the same thing to us. I know that the Spirit has to empower and change our hearts; I wonder if He might, in part do that by telling us to stop worrying about money and material things. He has done the work and everything is under control.

He has told us that He will take care of us and that it will be fine. He has told us to sell our possessions and give to the poor. In other words exchange what is less valuable for what is more valuable and quit being spending machine materialists.

Minority Rules

They see us as technological idolaters

Marshall McLuhan coined the term 'global village' but that is not what he is most famous for. He was a thinker, philosopher and writer who spoke to the issue of the medium being the message. He also thought a lot about man's creative bent. He said that every invention is an extension of some part of the human body. The phone, for example, is an extension of both the mouth and the ear. The automobile is an extension of the leg. The Internet is an extension of the leg, the eyes, the mouth and the ear etc. How about a microwave? An extension of our ability to rub two sticks together. You get the idea.

Man has devised ways to make life easier and to extend the limited human frame that we find ourselves in. On some levels that really is good news. McLuhan applauded innovation, but cautioned us against overextension of innovation, which can actually be harmful to society and the individual. Now some might say, "Wait a minute! These are time saving devices!" Saving time for what? I might ask. When mom used to make dinner in the kitchen we would hang around and talk and then do dishes by hand together. Loading the dishwasher is a solitary experience.

Because we have cars we do not walk and as a nation we are overweight. Because we have phones, email and text messaging we do not meet with people face to face to tell them good news or bad. We do not "touch" or make eye contact or read facial expressions. We have fewer real relationships because we do not need to go to the store. EBay or Amazon can provide all we need while we are sitting alone in our homes. I can book my air tickets on line and I get a bonus for doing it without talking to anyone. In fact the airlines and most other companies do not want me to talk to them at all, hence the ubiquitous phone tree. "Press 1 if you need…" If I do happen to talk to someone from a company, their first answer will be to direct me to the web site.

So all of the technologies we find ourselves with have come at a cost; all of them. And because of that, we are hurting socially and emotionally. So what do we do? We establish social networks on the web. Facebook, Instagram, LinkedIn, and blogs have entered in to create community for people.

I have a blog site. It is not community for me though. I do run on the edge of danger by being a blogger because I can get caught up in my world. I can surf a bit, read a bit and then write a bit. Self contained. What that eco system lacks is feedback, input from other people, who care about me enough to say something that is real.

I often chat with people who read my blog who say, "I was going to post a response, but then I did not". Maybe they are shy about their writing skills, maybe they are afraid someone might respond to their post or they might be wrong. In almost all of the cases, the person verbally told me what they thought. That is interesting and helpful to think about. Sometimes, people need to feel presence in order to feel safe to say what is important. That is just the opposite of what you might think. Maybe being anonymous does not fill our need to be able to say what we need to say.

Being on the Internet does fulfill something though. The average time on Facebook per visit is over 20 minutes and Facebook records billions of U.S. page views in a month. Compare that to the number of people who read the pages of the bible or any other religious book like the Quran or Torah. In order to equal Facebook page views, every American adult would have to read over 200 pages of the Bible or some other religious book in a month. Now add to that watching TV, listening to music, going to movies, reading books and you can see that what McLuhan said is true. Innovation overextended has a cost and it is potentially harmful to the soul.

We have a need but we are attempting to meet it through technology. This idea was driven home to me on a trip to London. As we were walking in the Shoreditch area I noted some great graffiti on the walls.

One was a picture of a young boy who was of African descent. He was clearly malnourished, wearing only a loincloth, but he had an iPod. The caption simply said, "iNeed." I think the artist was saying that all the technology in the world couldn't give this boy what he really needs. He needs love, food, clothes, and a home. The iPod cannot provide the touch he needs from a mother who loves him or the guiding hand of a father to bring him up in the way he should go. He has the most technologically advanced personal device he can have and it does not meet his need. We can continue to invent, refine and improve communication devices, television, graphics and travel but we will never replace what we long for. In the kingdom, those devices have little value except as things that can be exchanged for what is valuable.

They see us as golden age dreamers

We think a lot about the golden years. Many Christians have a 401k or some type of retirement vehicle that we are putting money into, or wish we were putting money into. Although we really do not want to sacrifice living standard today for living standard tomorrow, most of us want to retire and not have to work or depend on others for income. I would not go so far as to say that retirement is not a biblical concept, but I would say that we focus on getting to it in a way that may give only a wink to the truths of scripture. "How will I more then make ends meet when I get older?" "How much do I need and how do I plan?" A whole industry has evolved around Christian financial planning with part of it focused on retirement. It is difficult to weigh all the ends of the topic but perhaps we need to re-think money and frame it in a simple way.

If I spent less, I would save more or give more. Those are the only buckets I have to put money in. Spend, save, or give. Each of them has after effects. If I spend, it is either for a durable or non-durable good or service. In most cases spending is for things we will consume. If I save, I am forgoing present pleasure for something in the future. Oddly, that is true with giving. What I do invest in is what I think will bring pleasure or dividends down the road.

Minority Rules

The question may be "What is the highest use, or better put, the "sweetest use" of money?" I think Jesus would say to give some, maybe even a lot, of it to the poor so they can have something. If all things are created by Him and for Him, then should we believe, "there is more where that came from" or that He will figure out a new way to provide for our needs if we use up what we have? It seems to me we are trusting a bit more in money than in God. I do think we should save for the inevitable rainy day, but I wonder if that is really what we are saving it for.

What about our time and talents? Give some, even a lot, of them to the poor. Teach people who know less then you and then He will teach you more and you can do it again. Give it away. That is the heart of discipleship.

My church, Perimeter, tends to do that well under the leadership of Randy Pope, who for years has labored in the lives of men, teaching them to pass it along. The movie "Pay it Forward" clicked in the consciousness of Americans because people want to have good done to them and if they think good will come around again, they are willing to give up what they have.

A radical thought to most of us is to work out a theology of aging parents and the commandment to love and honor our mother and father. It seems that the bible says my children should help me when I get old. Maybe even let me live with them and not stick me in a retirement home, even if I can afford that. That seems to be a possibility the gospel affords me. The world is on a different track that I encourage us not to get on. It goes like this, "save money for me to spend on me when I get old." I know that is a hard statement.

I am not against any of us having money so that we can give our labors away for free if needed, but I think that we may need to look at what "over 65" looks like from a biblical perspective. And in every case the world is watching to see how we Christians hoard what we have even as we speak of helping the poor.

They see us as brown

I have a friend who is not a Christian. He made a great statement to me. He said he moved away from religion because religion is so dogmatic. Then he went on to share with me how Christians and the western world, although we are a minority of the world's population use the majority of the natural resources of the world including electricity, water, oil and minerals. I think our attitude may be "there is more where that came from and if not scientists will figure out a way to make something happen." The first part of that will not be true forever. There are a limited amount of resources, but scientists could find a way. Soylent Green for example. Scientific breakthroughs aside, the issue is how we spend the resources we have. In other words, if I spent less on energy, would that leave me resources to spend on other things that perhaps someone else could benefit from?
Christians are, on average, behind the green curve. I do not think there has ever been a survey done comparing the EPA MPG estimates for Christian's versus non Christian's vehicles. I could guess that they are about the

same in America. Try energy efficient water heaters, homes or types of clothes we buy, and my guess is we would be on par with everyone else.

I am convinced 150 years from now; Christians will look back on us and say, "What were they thinking? Driving big cars and funding through oil money the growth of other worldviews? Did they not see the connection? Did they not get it when the church began to sell properties that had been bled for to the Muslims so they could turn them into a mosque or to businessmen so they could turn them into a restaurant?"

I know that becoming green has a lot of scariness to it. Man does have dominion over animals and plants and I understand those who would say we should not let a small frog or owl prevent us from getting resources we need. I am simply stating that we can do more to preserve than we have. Others outside of our movement look at us as those who care little. It is something to think about.

They see us as hypocritical followers of Jesus

A man named Matthew wrote a short work in which he details much of the public life of Jesus. I highly recommend it if you have never read it. In chapters five, six and seven, he records a speech Jesus made to his followers. In the speech, Jesus has much to say about a lot of topics, and it is a wonderful prescription for how to live in a healthy way. In fact it is counter intuitive to say the least.

Minority Rules

He covers a lot of ground; everything from having mercy to persecution to being salt and light. He also talks about the downsides of anger, adultery and divorce. Good stuff and very helpful to anyone.

Then He seems to go to a whole new level. He talks about loving your enemy and giving to those who have needs. He mentions fasting and prayer, and He reminds us not to judge. That is hard because it is a national pastime. I am not just talking about in politics, business and with neighbors, but in Christendom.

We judge other brothers and sisters of different theological persuasions left and right. The prosperity gospel is really all about getting money isn't it? Baptists really think they choose God don't they? Presbyterians are frozen in time and space and do not have a compassionate bone in their body do they? People are suffering and we wear theology on our chest like a badge of honor sniffing, "Thank God I have arrived at the right point of view!" Judge not, or you too will be judged…and with the measure you use. When I read those words I think, "Let me rewind and take back some of those remarks I made about Joel Osteen." God forgive me. I am a hypocrite.

Jesus begins to close out the teaching by saying, "Get vertical with your talk and horizontal with your actions. Ask me, seek me and knock on my door. Then, take what I give you and give it away to your neighbors because you would want them to give something to you if they had something from me!"

Minority Rules

If I had been there, the rest of the conversation might have gone something like this:

Jesus: "Put this stuff into practice. That will be the sign that you really are a follower of mine and that the Holy Spirit really has taken up residence in your life. I am expecting some fruit, some evidence that you are who you claim to be: a Christian. Words won't suffice. Actions count. A life well lived counts. Struggle counts.

I know you can't do it perfectly, but you have to admit, I have given you a seed of faith *and* I have given you free will. Don't tell me you can't. The truth of the matter is you often just don't want to; you won't. The biggest issue for you is that you do not believe you have power from on high. You have it. And to say you don't is tantamount to calling me a liar. I love you and I want you to be healthy and to do the things that bring joy. The way I work that out is for you to choose to do what is right. When you fail: repent and I will give you more faith to live."

Randy: "Lord, why don't you just fully change my heart so I can be perfectly obedient and walk in your ways?"

Jesus: "I am not answering that question, even though it is a good one. I can tell you I have the best plan for My name, My kingdom and you. In your heart you know that. I can also tell you that when you die, you will be made perfect. This life is for a season and a reason. It is a life of wrestling with sin and the world and Satan. It is also a life of glimpses of glory and building of the kingdom. You see that from time to time don't you? You have to admit, that as you wrestle, fail, repent and get a touch more of grace, you see even more your need for Me don't you? When you get a glimpse of glory, you long for more don't you? So it is helpful to that end. I want you to know the depth of your sin, the sweetness of my heart to save you and the majesty of my glory. I could do it all at once, but you could not take it. This process will serve you well for all eternity as you look back on it. I will reveal more to you in the ages to come. For now, press on! Believe me and strive for holiness. You really are doing well. I love you and am for you."

Randy: "Thanks for clearing that up. I really am a hypocrite. I will ask You more often for faith to believe and live differently."

They see us as whiny protesters

We are known for being "against." We are against homosexuals, against abortion, against a moment of silence in public schools and against various other social activities that the majority wants. Now you might say that we are really "for" the opposite, but let's focus on how the world sees us and how we might better position ourselves. They want gay unions, abortion and prostitution? They see that as good for them. Nothing will convince them otherwise and trying to legislate morality for them just exacerbates the relational gap we already have. We do not believe in those things and other things the world wants because we think they are harmful to our souls and dishonoring to God. So we should believe that we will be better off for not participating. Our Christian community should shine in the midst of a society that is doing allegedly harmful things to itself shouldn't it?

Now I know it is a slippery slope here. Who will speak out on behalf of women sold into sex slavery or those who are victims of drunk drivers? We will and should, but that does not mean that we will win the vote in the next legislative session. We are a minority and the majority rules.

Are we "against" because we think they will gain more power as they indulge in activities we think wrong or are we against because they are an affront to God?

Do you think the people of the world will be worse off if they continue down the road of abortion, prostitution and gambling? If so, maybe it is better to take the perspective of Alcoholics Anonymous. At the end of the day, a drunk has to hit bottom. We should not be afraid that the decisions of the world will lead them to long range success. Is it that we are afraid they will be successful, or that they will damage us? Doesn't that say something about the apparent impotency of our beliefs?

Life choices can lead to spiritual awakening. Those who do not believe in Christ will either see that at some point or they won't. Our belief system says that the Holy Spirit has to alert them to the fact that He is real. Until then, they will act like they act and no amount of legislating morality will be helpful to their eternal souls. So one position could be to let all hell break loose and see what God does with it. Those who have really listened to the law of God and entered into His rest have done well in the long run spiritually, emotionally, psychologically and even financially.

Let me draw a line here lest you think I capitulate and am saying, "Everyone do what is right in your own eyes!" Should Wilberforce have fought to legislate an end the slave trade? Yes, he was a politician. That was his role and in that case another human being was involved. Should we work to end legalized abortion? Yes, because babies should have the right to choose. How about prostitution? Yes, we should fight that too. Am I contradicting myself here? I hope not. My point is that as we work to rid the world of what we see as unhealthiness, we should know that in a democratic society, the majority rules.

We are the minority and as such we will not win too many votes. That could oddly be to the detriment of those who do win the votes. In the mean time, our healthy community, which is doing healthy things, should be growing in a healthy way. There will come a time when we will need to really draw some hard lines. As a minority, we will need help from other minorities to able to do that. The lines will be about protecting our ability to worship, determining community membership and deciding ordinances of the church and who should receive them.

Questions to Ponder

1. How do you think materialism has gripped the Christian community at Christmas time? What could you do differently to be countercultural?

2. In what ways has technology been helpful to you? Discuss the benefits and costs of technology to your way of life.

3. Being "green" is often seen as "Democratic and Californian" type of initiative. What do you think about ecology? Why is it easy to talk about and hard to do? If you do not recycle, why don't you?

4. How can Christians avoid being labeled as, "Those people who are against everything"?

Chapter Four
How we got here

"I can't explain myself, I am afraid, because I am not myself you see!"   Alice, Alice in Wonderland

The world sees us as impotent bureaucrats. Our religion calls us to live as radicals. I think it would be good for us to admit that they may be right; we don't live as beautiful radicals. When we admit that, we will be able to look with a clearer lens at history and see what has really happened to our movement. That will enable us to look and see what is to come and where we are going. Scarlet O'Hara asked Rhett Butler, "What will become of us?" Our answer is not, "Frankly dear, I don't give a damn." What will become of us is yet to be revealed and I have great hope for our movement. We are going some place good. To get there, we need to get a bit of an historical overview of where we have come from.

Not that you agree with all of my observations but you may agree enough with some of them to ask "What brought us here and how do we move from here?" Furthermore you might ask, "Where is this all going? What will become of us? Is there a growth spurt in the future of the American church? Will Jesus come back while everything is a mess to buy low?"

Well He will come back, but the timing is far beyond the scope of this book or any other I know and He won't buy low, because He has already made His purchases. So we are left with the other questions. How did we get here? I think we can find the answer by looking across the pond. We got here by two hundred years of the church not being the church, but by it being a mostly silent bystander to great historical events thereby being co-opted into them and changed by them.

Many of us in America can trace our roots to Europe. Although we have large groups who emigrated willingly or unwillingly from China, Africa and other places, the founding fathers came from Great Britain. Our short 250-year heritage is intertwined with theirs, like it or not. The English, Scots, Welsh and Irish have a long history with religion. Great Britain is a small nation that has had a large impact on the spread of Christianity around the world. The gospel came early and stayed. Then Henry the VIII decided that he wanted to "do his own thing" and the Church of England was born. That was a defining moment for the church. Henry settled the question of who had ultimate authority: he did. And the church became an agent of the state.

At the same time, the English were generally whipping up on other people around the world and establishing the British Empire. As part of that process they took along their culture and religion, which happened to be Christianity. Australia got it, as did parts of Africa through Livingston, India through Carey and Stanley, and America through Whitefield and Edwards.

So the empire that never saw the sun set on it took Christianity right along with it. But those who held to ancient Christianity were marginalized for the sake of political and economic power. Christianity was seen as the part of the culture they took along with them which separated them from the heathen. It was one of the reasons they thought themselves superior. Christianity became a tool of the empire and power corrupted those who used it.

An overview of British history is far beyond the scope of this book, I only bring it up to show in some sense that we are viewed as a marginalized group because we watched as history took place and, other than a few noble martyrs, we sat silent as leaders both in business and government did as they wished, *while calling themselves Christians.* The empire became more important than the kingdom of God. It was more tangible. Over time the kingdom of God began to be seen as a nuisance as opposed to a help to the expansion of the empire. When religion mixes with the state, the state wins and religion morphs to become a tool of the state. That happened in England.

From the time of Horatio Nelson's great victory at Trafalgar and for another hundred years Britain ruled the waves. But underneath the Christian veneer, the culture began to decay morally, politically and socially. Christians thought they were the majority, they compromised their values for power and subsequently lost their religion.

Men like Wilberforce, Carey, Taylor, Livingston and Stanley made a mark on society for the good of the Kingdom and the ripples were felt around the world. Their legacy, which was built on the legacy of the Wesley brothers and Whitefield, who in turn had built their legacy on the Puritans, Covenanters, Owen et al, who had rested on the shoulders of the Reformers would last a hundred years, but they would find no one to pass the baton on to.

By the time of Queen Victoria, the Christian society of the 1800's began to collapse. The next generation viewed it as stuffy, white shirt, starchy and boring. They were right. It was. Codified Christianity is not enticing. Christianity was not seen as a revolutionary religion. There was nothing exciting in going to church especially if it was high Anglican Church in an ancient cathedral.

After the turn of the century came two horrible world wars. It is hard to imagine how death and war sap the hope from a civilization. Although in many respects the British soldier was the backbone that did not break, his religion came out of it scathed with unanswered questions by clergy of how God could have permitted atrocities like the world should never have seen.

By the 1960s, it really was all over. The empire was gone and the British decided to open the doors of immigration in an effort to include those in the commonwealth for the sake of multiculturalism. As a result, tens of thousands immigrated to London from Pakistan, India and other former British colonies. The immigrants brought with them their culture. Unlike the great melting pot that America was in the early 1900's, the new arrivals did not assimilate. Why was this immigration different? The immigrants to America came from Catholic and Protestant lands and easily transitioned into a country with similar Catholic and Protestant roots. The immigrants to Britain came from countries where their religion was distinctively different. Muslims and Hindus came from Pakistan and India. Arabs began to arrive from Middle Eastern countries. Over the years, they worked hard to move up the economic ladder and they added to their numbers through birth and through the emigration of other family members. They were not met by a Christian culture because it had decayed. They were met by secularism and materialism.

Today, even though most people in Britain will check the survey box "Christian," only 5% go to church. Christians, long ago achieved tiny minority status in London. Islam is clearly the dominant religion while secular humanism has wrapped itself around the soul of the country and squeezed the gospel out of it. From a once rich literary, cultural, artistic and educated country now comes football hooliganism, third world cityscapes, reality TV and "Queen: The Musical, we will Rock you." Trash TV, trash newspapers and trash in the streets. It is heartbreaking to see. Not everywhere but many places. It reminds me a bit of the scene from the Lion King when Scar takes over and the landscape changes to desolate wasteland.

The Church of England's response seems to be to have a stiff upper lip and to close redundant churches. Currently there are hundreds of C of E churches that are no longer needed for worship. At the same time the multi-culturalism policies of politicians in the 1970s through

Minority Rules

1990s have developed into a problem that was not anticipated. Immigrants are not assimilating into society; they are demanding that society change, so Prince Charles could become defender of faith, not *the* faith.

I do believe God is at work in the midst of this seeming chaos. What I think I see happening is that God providentially decreed the British Empire to never see the sun set on it for a time, in order that the empire would have colonies on every continent in the world, in order that there would be a Commonwealth, in order that there would be British educational systems in place around the world, in order that people would learn, in order that London would become the financial and banking capital of the world, in order that immigration policies would be loosened and people from the Commonwealth, as well as the European Union, would come to London, in order that the gospel might be preached to them in English by brave souls who will take it back to their home countries over the next ten years.

Odd that He would do it that way. I could be wrong, but I like the thought. And I know that was a long sentence.

The path is not that clear and clean however. The church is weak in England, so immigrants are pouring in and are overwhelming the system. They are changing society to their way of living, thinking and playing. Laws are being established that will make it harder to preach the gospel in public. To re-establish the church in England will take great expense and brave men and women. In the mean time, Islam is on the ascendancy in England. All signs point to Islam becoming the primary religion of the country.

Will America follow down the footpath of England? Yes, I think so. Our immigration policies are similar, our Christian roots have long since been pulled up and we have little ability to speak to the issue of absolute truth. So all newcomers and anyone with a point of view are "right" and have rights. Christians have been fighting skirmishes over prayer in public schools and Ten Commandments in courthouses while mosques have been built in major cities and Muslims are being elected. I do not begrudge that. I think the state can and should reflect the population. The point is, how are those who are religious to be distinct from the state? Have Christians fully assimilated and should we learn from those groups who have not?

Recently the British government has begun to understand the tremors underground. They see that religion may be a dividing point that would cause adherents to not assimilate into the culture. In fact, by definition that should be happening. If the culture is secular in nature, true believers should be in some ways distinctive. For Muslims, that could be that they eat halal meat, wear the Hijab, take Friday off, and fast during Ramadan. What might that be for Christians? Some might say it is the wearing of the cross. Could be. Should all Christians wear a cross? How about not working on Sundays? Eating fish on Friday? What is it that makes the Christian "noticeable" on the street? The reality is none of the above. Christians are called to love even their enemies.

Minority Rules

Their love is to be so radical that it is noticeable. That is what makes a Christian distinctive.

Our movement lost the heart of the gospel in Britain. Christians should have conducted their affairs quietly and set a priority on Kingdom business. That would have meant stewardship, work ethic, desire to live a simple life and give generously especially to the household of believers. Christians should have been creators of jobs and wealth as well as distributors of the gospel. Christians should have been educated and serious about gaining more education. They should have been leading in fields of research, literature, medicine etc. In other words they should have been fulfilling the creation mandate. Instead our recent ancestors began to live off the fat of the land and we inherited the malaise. Most importantly, they began to look to the world, not to Christ to meet their needs.

I do not mean to point a finger here without noticing where the thumb is pointing. We are no better. I am no better. We all could do better. We look to the world and not to Christ and we cannot fully blame those who have come before us. Our great hope is to learn from minorities and look to Him as we go forward because one day soon our position will truly be visible to the world and we need to be prepared to live in the full light of our minority status.

Questions to ponder

1. Do you think that the situation in Europe is a predictor of things to come in America? Why or why not? Can you give examples?

2. How do you think Christians can live in society and not get "changed" by it? How can you change society?

3. What do you think of religious symbols and customs? Are they helpful to a religion? Would you use or wear a symbol? Why?

4. In what ways do you think Christians have co-opted holidays and lifestyle to American society?

Minority Rules

Minority Rules

Chapter Five
Learning from minorities

"I do not pray for success, I ask for faithfulness"
                                        Mother Teresa

So, by now you might be getting the sense that I think our movement will decline further in America as immigrants bring new religion here as they did in Britain and as we meander along the road to power discarding the truth of our religion. Some of you may be saying, "About time you recognized it, maybe now you Christians can quit being so arrogant" Well said. Others of you may be saying, "So, how do we become the majority?" Someone else will have to write that book. A few of you may be asking the question, "Can you give us a picture of a minority movement that could be helpful?" Glad you asked. I think so, and I think God in His gentleness has given us other minority groups to look at to see what is helpful and what is not. I will first state a few overarching thoughts and then give a few specific examples.

How minorities believe

I have come to learn that accomplishments are driven by beliefs. In other words I will *do* what I believe. I can say I believe something, but if my actions don't follow, I really do not believe it. It is that "faith without works is dead" thing that James wrote about. For example I can say I want to spend time with my kids, but if my calendar does not reflect it, I really do not believe I should spend time with my kids. If I believed, then I would act. I might not act perfectly, but at least I would in proportion to the strength of my belief.

Jonathan Edwards the great British theologian wrote a wonderful work called *Religious Affections.* In the book he describes how we as humans have inclinations or "affections" which cause us to act the way we do. Every action has an underlying or motivating affection that prompted it. By looking at the actions of a man, we can often see what he believes.

Another way of looking at it is from the perspective of language. What you say, and the language you use, both shapes what you believe and is indicative of what you actually believe. The early church had a name for this. They called it "Lex orandi, Lex credendi" in Latin which means, "The Law of prayer is the Law of belief." In other words, what people pray reveals what they believe and in fact informs their beliefs. That is why the church for so many years refused to pray extemporaneously. Prayers and creeds were written so as to accurately reflect doctrine and teach congregants what to believe in the hopes that their actions would follow.

The same holds true in Islam. The Quran can only be read in Arabic and the Hadith teaches people what to believe by saying it for them. No deviations are allowed because to allow them could promote doctrinal shifts.

All minorities believe what they actually do. The more passionately they do it, the more authentic their beliefs. If they only speak about it, but do not do it, they really do not believe it. So, the question for all of us is, "Do we really believe?" Everyone subscribes to a worldview, but that does not mean they live it. In fact there may be a million different worldviews that in a syncretistic way create personal belief systems. There is the Randy Schlichting worldview, which is mostly Christian but adds in secular humanism, hedonism etc. Not to say I am not a Christian. That is a state that was chosen for me by another but the point is that I do not act like a Christian because I often am overwhelmed by the dust of unbelief, which causes me to act, not like the adopted son that I am, but like an orphan.

John Calvin talks about the challenge Christians have. Basically, they have some faith, but the "dust of unbelief" remains and can in fact "collect" on the soul of a man and eventually cause him to not live what he may have believed. It is incumbent on leaders to help shake the dust of unbelief from the souls of followers.

Minorities who are true to their values really do live out their beliefs. They act upon what they believe to be true and those around can see that they are living what they believe. Amish. Orthodox Jews. Some Muslims. Green Bay Packer cheese heads. They live what they believe and it shows.

How minorities think

A mind is a terrible thing to waste. Healthy minority groups mentally focus with the intensity of a laser beam. It makes sense. If you are committed to your cause, then you are spending all of your waking hours thinking about how to advance it. You do not want to get caught up in the affairs of the day or world. Focus is the operative word.

One of my favorite fictional characters is Sherlock Holmes. Arthur Conan Doyle wrote brilliant stories of the famous detective, weaving mystery and action together like few others. I learned a lesson about how minorities think by reading "The Scarlet Letter." In this early work, Dr Watson and Holmes are classmates at university and Watson discovers how Holmes thinks:

"He was not studying medicine. He had himself, in reply to a question, confirmed Stamford's opinion upon that point. Neither did he appear to have pursued any course of reading which might fit him for a degree in science or any other recognized portal, which would give him an entrance into the learned world. Yet his zeal for certain studies was remarkable, and within eccentric limits his knowledge was so extraordinarily ample and minute that his observations have fairly astounded me. Surely no man would work so hard or attain such precise information unless he had some definite end in view. Desultory readers are seldom remarkable for the exactness of their learning. No man burdens his mind with small matters unless he has some very good reason for doing so.

His ignorance was as remarkable as his knowledge. Of contemporary literature, philosophy and politics he appeared to know next to nothing. Upon my quoting

Minority Rules

Thomas Carlyle, he inquired in the naivest way who he might be and what he had done. My surprise reached a climax, however, when I found incidentally that he was ignorant of the Copernican Theory and of the composition of the Solar System. That any civilized human being in this nineteenth century should not be aware that the earth traveled round the sun appeared to me to be such an extraordinary fact that I could hardly realize it.

"You appear to be astonished," he said, smiling at my expression of surprise. "Now that I do know it I shall do my best to forget it."

"To forget it!"

"You see," he explained, "I consider that a man's brain originally is like a little empty attic, and you have to stock it with such furniture as you choose. A fool takes in all the lumber of every sort that he comes across, so that the knowledge, which might be useful to him, gets crowded out, or at best is jumbled up with a lot of other things, so that he has a difficulty in laying his hands upon it. Now the skilful workman is very careful indeed as to what he takes into his brain-attic. He will have nothing but the tools, which may help him in doing his work, but of these he has a large assortment, and all in the most perfect order. It is a mistake to think that that little room has elastic walls and can distend to any extent. Depend upon it there comes a time when for every addition of knowledge you forget something that you knew before. It is of the highest importance, therefore, not to have useless facts elbowing out the useful ones."

Minority Rules

"But the Solar System!" I protested.

"What the deuce is it to me?" he interrupted impatiently: "you say that we go round the sun. If we went round the moon it would not make a pennyworth of difference to me or to my work."

I was on the point of asking him what that work might be, but something in his manner showed me that the question would be an unwelcome one. I pondered over our short conversation, however, and endeavoured to draw my deductions from it. He said that he would acquire no knowledge, which did not bear upon his object. Therefore all the knowledge which he possessed was such as would be useful to him…"

> Quoted from "A Study in Scarlet" by Sir Arthur Conan Doyle

I love that passage because I aspire to it and think we all should. Useless information is useless. Trivia is trivial. We retain information about football statistics, celebrities and reality TV at the cost of something.

Minorities stuff into their "brain attic" only what is useful to the cause. They have no room for frivolities and their leadership keeps them focused.

How minorities live

I may get myself into trouble here because I am going to make some generalizations. As a good mathematician will tell you there are standard deviations and variances,

Minority Rules

so please take a look at the framework and see if it fits in general terms. As much as possible I will focus on the Christian minority.

Most people saw the movie, "My Big Fat Greek Wedding" a classic tale of a minority family living in America. Great Greek food, wine, traditions, colors and rituals abounded in the household. They were Americans but they were also Greek and they did not forget it. Their traditions kept them in touch with the past, in touch with who they were. Every minority has traditions that it not just clings to but, enjoys and even reveres. Muslims have Halal food and conservative dress; Italians great wine and pasta; Jews Hanukah; and the Scots have Hogmanay.

Healthy minorities band together and give sacrificially in order to accomplish their objectives. They live a simple life and they work together for the sake of the cause. They forego luxuries and give all they can for the movement to be successful and for the next generation to take further hold. They spend their money on the cause; not on extraneous items.

Strong minorities act out their beliefs. I have a friend who loves animals and healthy eating. She combines both of those to be an activist for the cause. She researches, she writes and she makes well thought through presentations about her passion. She is all about the cause.

Some, who are members of a minority movement, just live it out. I had a friend who went to work with Mother Teresa. It was during monsoon season and every day it rained, until the streets of Calcutta were flooded. If you have never been to India it will be hard to describe the scene. The big cities of India are overrun with poverty and more poverty. Putrid and stench are good words to begin to describe the picture. The spiritual, moral and social depravity is so tangible that you are assaulted through all five of your senses at the same time. It is overwhelming.

My friend chose to work there as an aide in the home for the dying. The sisters at the home pick people up off the street; lepers, beggars, prostitutes and they bring them to the home so they can die with dignity. My friend stayed close to the home and every day she would wade through the flooded streets with garbage, rats, and human waste floating next to her just to get to the place she was serving. After weeks, she was mentally, physically, emotionally and spiritually exhausted.

One day, she was sitting next to the bed of a man who was close to death and she started to weep (I do as I write this). He was dying; nothing could be done for him. He was a minority, one of the untouchable beggars. She just wept. All of a sudden she felt a hand on her shoulder. She turned to see who it was and through tear soaked eyes she saw Mother Teresa. Mother was not looking at her; she was gazing with a wonderful smile at the man who was dying. She said nothing to my friend and my friend turned back to gaze at the man too. He died with dignity. In a city of twenty million mostly Hindus and Muslims two Christian women were loving him well; two minority women just living out their beliefs.

Minority Rules

How minorities can impact culture

Now I may really get myself in trouble. I am going to talk about the gay rights movement. They are a great example of how the minority can impact the majority in terms of culture, art and law. Research shows that about 4% of Americans are gay. That is clearly a minority. Yet in the last twenty years they have been able to normalize the gay life style, inject it into television, radio and movies and move to have laws passed recognizing marriage between same sex couples. They have also brought the AIDS pandemic to the highest point on the radar screen. How did they do all of that? They are focused on their cause. In the case of AIDS it is a life or death struggle. They have tapped into the American psyche in the area of justice. If Americans stand for anything it is justice. We love a good court case and we want people to get what they justly deserve. We do not want them to be greedy and get more then they deserve, but we do want people to get what is fair, particularly in the area of human rights. I think that is part of the DNA of Americans.

Our nation was birthed from a struggle with a king who would not give us our rights. We have this inalienable sense that vocal people in a sense "earn" their rights.

Strong minorities are also determined to use the legal system to their advantage. Thanks to our great system of government, which really is amazing, we have three branches with checks and balances. (This is a High School civics review moment). The legislative makes the laws, the executive enforces the laws and the judicial interprets the laws. That is all very good. The challenge is that the legislative is made up of people, the executive is made up of people and the judicial is made up of people. You can tell me all you want that we need to keep church and state separate and I will say that if you mean the institutions, the answer is yes. If you mean the people, the answer is that is impossible. Everyone has a worldview and they all bring it to the table as they make decisions. So those who write laws do so from their point of view as to how the world should be. Those who execute the laws will do so in a way that is culturally familiar to them. And those who interpret the laws will for sure interpret through their own lens of experience, worldview and culture even in light of the Constitution.

So, as minority groups move to America, or Britain or wherever, they become politically active and begin to vote for people who believe what they believe. And when those people become the legislature, they make laws that reflect who they are.

Oratory and rhetoric combined with political and legal action begins to normalize a minority group's position, however non-main stream it may be. Remember Lex Orandi? As we speak, so we shall believe. Smart minorities know that to be true and so they speak loudly and often.

I was at Speakers Corner in Hyde Park, London one day. It is one of the few places in the world that people can speak and debate freely. Every Sunday afternoon people bring their soapbox (literally a step stool), get up on it, and express their views. The crowd, which can be quite sizable, either listens to or debates with the speaker. Dozens of people are on step stools trying to make their case for their worldview. It is fascinating. By the way I think it should be on your list of ten things you want to do before you die because everyone I have ever taken has been changed by the experience. On this particular day, a Muslim on the stepladder said, "I believe that Britain would be better off if we had Sharia law!" Interesting thought. Oratory with action begins to change society. Outrageous? Maybe not.

When people begin speaking about things, however outrageous, impossible or initially wrong they seem, over time, people begin to say, "Well why not?" We have seen it with the Civil Rights movement, the Gay Rights movement and the Pro Choice movement. Why not?

Unhealthy Minority Moves

Before we take a look at some minority movements that have lessons to be learned within them, I want to say a word about unhealthy minorities and their approach to life.

There is a lot of pain and suffering in this world and minorities have really been the victims of much of it. They have been beaten, marginalized, disenfranchised and "'caste'igated". By that word (which I just invented) I mean that in every society there is an unspoken caste system. The one in India just happens to be above the watermark and is therefore visible to the world. In every society there are people at the bottom of the heap, who are uneducated, underemployed and unable to climb the ladder. Part of their lot in life has been caused by those who are above them.

Over a cycle that is somewhat predictable, frustration builds up within the minority community, a leader emerges and a press is made on the majority for rights. Typically, the majority does not want to give the minority anything because guess what? It comes from their pocket, or so they think. "If I give him more, I will have less."

So the majority resists change; sometimes very successfully and sometimes not so successfully. At times those on top are smart enough to change their form so that people think they are giving the minority freedom. At the end of the day, the minority either accepts the "new status quo" or they revolt in civil disobedience or in civil war. The case in Egypt in 2011 to 2013 had shadows of this idea.

Some minority groups approach problem solving in an inhumane way. Bombing, kidnapping and other terror activities have rarely resulted in moving forward the aims of a minority group in any real way. Sadly, the dark heart of man continues to think that explosions will lead to explanations and nothing could be further from the truth.

But there have been through out history, and are even today, some healthy minority movements. And we can learn from those movements.

Minority Rules

Untouchables and Christianity in India

World history is fascinating. You can see how one thing led to another and another and how the "invisible Hand" connected the dots. Take India for example. For thousands of years they were "unto themselves" and had developed a religious system incorporating caste as a way of life and death. Along came the British with the bad news of the East India Trading Company and the good news of William Carey. Both hit the shores in the 1800's and the East India Trading Company, because it was introduced by force, "stuck" for a hundred years or so. Then along came Mohandas Gandhi.

I have spent quite a bit of time in India and one thing I have walked away with is the knowledge that Gandhi is known by all and revered by many. In fact he was given the title "Mahatma" which means "Great Soul." He was a determined man with a vision to help the lot of the untouchables and he was willing to go to extremes to achieve it. He employed non-violent resistance to change the minds of those who were violent and in the majority.

Perhaps he would have said, "When the majority (and it does not always take sheer numbers to have majority power if you have weapons) overwhelms you by their size, and strength, you have to choose a different path to victory than force!" He did, and the majority was moved. Other authors have written well about Gandhi and he is not without his critics. I would suggest spending time researching his life and times further for those who are interested. At the end of the day, Indians achieved independence from Great Britain. Gandhi gave his life in the process.

This mega movement of Gandhi created a lot of shockwaves. The waves of the partition in 1947 of India and Pakistan were followed by the partition of the partition into Pakistan and Bangladesh with Muslims moving one way and Hindus the other in an attempt to be the majority. Underneath this movement was the movement of the true minority in India. Christianity. That is what Christians were and are in India; *the* minority. As Hindu nationalism grows and Islam rises in India, Christianity is seen as a threat to the majority.

Christians in India know they are a minority and they live like it for the most part. They are creating by the power of the Holy Spirit healthy Christian communities that are making a difference in the slums of Mumbai, Nagpur and other places. If you want to get a good look at it, spend some time with my friend Nittin Sardar and Din Bandhu ministries. They make a difference in people's lives for the sake of the gospel.

Islam

Islam started less than 1500 years ago in the desert town of Medina with Mohammed and a few followers. Now it boasts almost 25% of the population of the world; an amazing success story. In many countries they have moved from minority to majority status and in several countries they have moved to being the exclusive religion. What propelled this? The founder of Islam had a focused mission. He lived simply and devoted time and resources to the main thing he desired. And he had grand success because of it.

Today, Muslims are transforming major cities all around the world. They have what we would call a saturation mosque planting strategy. I can see evidence of that when I go to London and other cities where they have immigrated. There are several reasons for this I think. They tend to pick urban settings where there is public transportation and easy pedestrian access. Schools, jobs and homes are in close proximity to one another. Even in the suburbs they tend to choose higher density areas. Secondly, because of the mandate for prayer five times a day, people are drawn to the mosque. They need to live close by, which enables them to get to know one another and causes socialization to happen. Shopkeepers begin to understand the new demographics of the area and they purchase for resale the types of goods their neighbors like. Signs may change to Arabic, newspapers become available that have a Muslim point of view and so on. They look, act and work as a people group.

Today, in other parts of the world, Muslims are a minority and they for the most part do a good job of acting like it. They are sober minded and diligent in their pursuit of solidifying and preserving their community. But, they do not stop there. They have a growth strategy. Part of it has to do with conversion, but much more of it has to do with procreation, especially in the developing world. Now I am not making an absolute case here. Some Muslims are marginal in there beliefs no doubt but the general pattern seen is a group of people who adhere to their religious principles.

ISIS

It is hard for an author to talk about ISIS in a positive light. I know Jesus says "love your enemy" so I have to; but I dislike what they do. You, like me, might think they are wrong in their tactics and in their fundamental worldview, which points them in the direction they are running.

But can we learn from them? They are a minority who vehemently believes the majority is wrong and they are doing something about it. Their goal is world domination and they are willing to sacrifice everything for their goal; even their lives.

Think about that for a minute. Can you imagine being involved in a movement that so convinces you, that you believe in so much, that you think that giving up your life for it is well worth the price? They must be fools or they must be right. There is no in-between here. They live in caves and on the run, giving no thought to conveniences of modern life, save what will help them accomplish their mission. They do not have a retirement plan and they are not planning a vacation any time soon.

I am not saying, "Well, we should respect them for the way they live out what they believe." I do say that we can learn something. Jesus calls us to die to self, not blow ourselves up in planes. And that means for us to live like the coming of the kingdom is of more value than our very lives, possessions and even families. The coming of the King is of supreme value.

Early Christians

Our movement has traditionally held minority status. The Israelites were a very small people group. Even during the reign of David and Solomon, they were not a dominant power in the Middle East. The early church was certainly a minority and even after the "nationalization of religion" by Constantine in 313AD the true church remained small.

There have been pockets of time when the church was a majority in a city such as Geneva under Calvin or Kidderminster under Baxter. But for the most part though, we have not done well when we are the majority. Paradoxically we live more as freemen when we are the minority.

Catholics as a people group tend to be devoted and family oriented. The church universal has much to learn from our Catholic friends. The idea of the catholic parish has much merit and the schools and hospitals developed by Catholics have blessed the world.

Having said all that as a backdrop, we do have to address the issue of the Holy Roman Empire. Some might ask, "Wasn't that a time when Christians were a majority and ruled and isn't that the way it is supposed to be?"

Minority Rules

A good history reading will reveal that it was a co-regency with kings and others. The church never really dominated the world system. Christians are not meant to have a worldly empire here. We are called to be citizens of the kingdom of God and be agents in this world for Him.

It is so easy for me to read the book of Acts, and miss the point. Yes, it is a book about the power of the Holy Spirit indwelling the lives of people so that they speak boldly about Jesus. It is a book about the spread of the gospel from Jerusalem to Judea to Samaria to the uttermost parts of the world. It is not about Christians beginning a victorious march to majority rule. They were never, ever on the verge of transforming countries, cities or villages. That is not the intention of the gospel. The gospel transforms hearts that happen to live in countries, cities or villages.

So as I read the book of Acts now, I read it as a minority people group surviving in a hostile environment, and doing well as a community (except when they get beaten, thrown out of cities, left for dead and actually killed). They do not have much materially speaking, politically speaking and intellectually speaking. What they do have is a singular focus on what is important. They get the main thing for them: Christ, Him crucified and Him resurrected. That is it. That is all that matters to them and so they both "apologize" and "polemicize" for the rest of their lives. Anyone want to talk about sports, the Romans, the Egyptians, the latest fashion, the newest music? These guys could have cared less who was in power, what the political slogans were, and how the banking system might work with Roman coins. They focused on their passion, which was living for Christ as long as they lived.

That does not mean they were not politicians, bankers and lawyers. It means that they saw their work in light of their love of Christ. Our tendency is to love the fashion, coins and political news, which really translate into a hate for Christ. We cannot serve God and money. So we choose money.

So what is the bottom line here? We can learn from Muslims, Atheists and even those we might not vote for in an election. We don't need to attack them. They are not the problem. If God is in control of all things and he works all together then we as Christians should look around and see how He might be using other people to get to us. He did it in the Old Testament. He has done it throughout history. Their story is not another story. It is part of His and He wants us to look to them to get a clue about how He wants us to live.

Minority Rules

Questions to ponder

1. Pick one of the minority groups you are familiar with, or perhaps another that you are in, and discuss successful strategies they have used to move their agenda forward.

2. How do you think you can control information that is coming into your brain-attic and become more like Sherlock Homes, if you agree that is a good idea?

3. Where do your actions not line up with what you say you believe? This is a hard question to talk about. What would enable you to better live your beliefs? Will trying harder cause you to do better or is there a point where you say, "I give up!" What do you do then?

Chapter Six
Creating a Healthy Minority - Beginnings

"Every great idea eventually degenerates to a thing called work"

Randy Schlichting

How do we get there? How do we become a healthy minority? **First off, we need to remember that we are powerless to make it happen.** We need to beg God for a heart change and ask the Holy Spirit to push us where we cannot go by ourselves. Then we need to set a base from which we can work. A good and holy foundation is essential to having a healthy minority community.

Some foundational values that may guide us on the journey:

1. **Accept our minority status.** We are but a remnant. It is by God's design that we are. If we can own and wear that, we will have come a long way. We know Christ, the power of salvation and all other good things, because He knows us and that is the foundation. We are indeed His people.

2. **Don't pretend we are victims.** We need to own our dirt and freely admit that we are messed up. There is only one victim in our religion the God-Man Jesus Christ who was victimized at the hands of sinners. Sinners not just *like* us, but us. We are the perpetrators. All of us, who happen to have been shown the depth of our sin, and have

seen it, have become beneficiaries and we should be a heck of a lot more grateful than we are.

3. **Know truth and speak it.** This is a hard point to stick in here. It would be too easy to say, "Let's be nice and love people and mind our own business." The truth is, our business is the King's business and He died for sinners that they might repent and come to know Him as Lord. Hell is real and people who do not believe in Jesus will go there. It is the truth, so we should say so. A corollary to this is to not sit idly by and let people who are not really Christians call themselves Christians. If someone doesn't believe in penal, substitutionary atonement, they are not a real Christian. If they don't believe in the virgin birth? Not a Christian. Don't agree that Jesus was sinless? Not a Christian. We have had elastic boundaries for the church for too long. Tighten up. If you need help, re-read Jesus.

4. **Remember history.** We are not the first or last. We are people in the middle between His first coming and His second coming. Part of our responsibility is to leave the house in order for the next occupants. I have asked the question as others have, "What happened to England?" This was the land of John Knox, John Owen, Charles Spurgeon, Hudson Taylor, John Wesley, C.S. Lewis, and Horatio Bonar and today they have a population of 55 million with only 3 million attending church. They failed to pass the baton.

They failed to have kids. They got caught up in materialism. Today we have forgotten about the Godly heroes of yesteryear and we are overly enamored with the comic book heroes of man.

Additionally, we should support the heroes of our generation, men and women who pioneer ministry. We need to re-tell the stories of Jesus as our revolutionary leader by reading the Bible, believing that its words are powerful and transformative to those who believe, and those who are coming to faith.

Finally, and this is hard to say, there has been much written about saturation church planting over the last ten years. The word saturation could indicate to those who oppose us, a push towards majority. While I appreciate the heart behind the brothers and sisters who have a vision for this, I would ask that we look at the history of our movement and see how we are called to live as the church given our status. I wonder if a parish mindset might be the way to live as a healthy minority.

5. **Believe in the power of the resurrection** No other religion has the power of the resurrection. Hindus have the hope of reincarnation. Muslims have the possibility of favor, but only Christians have the power of the resurrection. I met a man on a plane while traveling to India. He asked me why I was going and I said to worship with

brothers and sisters in Mumbai. In reply he said, "You know we are all brothers and sisters. There is one God" Then he went on to give me an eloquent dissertation on Hinduism and glowingly recounted the life and times of his guru-ji. After fifteen minutes, I asked him about death. "We come back," he said as a matter of fact. It really was a neat and tidy system; all self contained. Everything just kept getting re-cycled. I asked him what he knew of Christianity. He said, "They go to church and they give money for schools and orphanages." As I walked through the gospel with him, he got stuck at the point of seeing that one child is born poor and one rich. In his mind that had to be because of the sins or good deeds of a prior life. I did not have what it took to convince him otherwise.

After I left him I thought about his view of coming back after you die. A friend I knew in India once prayed for someone to come back from the dead. As my friend told me that story, of praying for someone to be resurrected, I thought, "We in America never think to pray for someone to come back from the dead" and I wondered why. God can do that. Maybe we should cry out to Him more often. I do know that much more often, He raises a soul from death to life by spiritual re-birth. That is something we can believe in and we need to call out for more often and with great zeal.

Questions to ponder

1. Most people don't like studying history. They find it boring. Share about your interest in history and the idea that we are called to take a look back to see where we have been. What are some of the pitfalls to looking back at history though the eyes of others?

2. Can you discuss the last ten or twenty years of American history and the church in America? What do you think has happened? What does the future hold based on the recent past?

3. What does the term "power of the resurrection" mean to you?

4. How vocal should Christians be about the core doctrines of the faith when talking to those outside the faith? How about those who are Christians, but of other denominational affiliations?

Minority Rules

Chapter Seven
Minority Rules

So what will it take? How do we go about uncovering what it means to live as a healthy minority? I have purposely said nothing to this point about the church of which I am a member, but I do want to say here that I think we at Perimeter are on a track to live out our minority status and live by the rules. I have been blessed to work with men and women who are passionate like crocodile hunters, serve like nuns in India and continue to beg God for humility to see their sin and their need for Him. We are a group who often know how messy we are. We hurt one another, we are selfish and we are not what we want to be. We are a mixed lot. As I unpack the rules, I want you to know that we kind of live them some of the time. Sometimes we do not, because we are sinners.

Now for a rule to be worth keeping, it has to empower. If it restricts or diminishes, it will not be kept for long and it will not energize those who attempt to keep it.

Rules are principles born from convictions. Rules define statements like "Here are the things we *always* strive to do; things that give us energy" or "Here are the things we *never* want to do and in fact we try hard not to do because if we do them we are diminished." Rules are better kept if they are things that people want to do, not things that people begrudgingly have to do. Motivation goes a long way to help people keep rules. Most people hate rules because they see them as constricting. We do not mind them when they apply to other people because

Minority Rules

in that case they are of benefit to us but we would prefer to not be tied down ourselves. Bluntly put, that is the heart of sin. When we are above the rules we are saying we are God.

Fortunately, deep down in our souls, God has implanted the idea that rules are helpful to us. We get sideways with rules because we believe we have to work to keep them and it often seems that the energy required to keep them outweighs the benefits. I want to encourage you to take a deep breath and try to set aside that word picture of rules because it is a worldly paradigm.

The kingdom does not work on energy and effort. It works by the power of the Spirit. So if you are finding yourself worn out, you are not living the gospel. And you may be keeping the wrong rules or trying to keep the right ones by your own power. It cannot be done. Rule keeping in the kingdom is not heavy or burdensome. Even though we will not always keep the rules, it is not always a lack of effort that causes our failure. It is lack of faith. And we can not manufacture that.

A kingdom rule acts as a guideline. It is a pathway that is wide enough for variations within the theme. There is a narrow gate to enter into the path of the Kingdom, but once in, the Spirit broadens and even makes less rocky the path so that both the weak and the strong can walk along. Wrecks can still occur if we have the wrong man guiding us, but if we listen and appropriate what has been given us, we can worshipfully head down the path and be blessed by the rules.

Minority Rules

Jonathan Edwards is one of my heroes. Over the course of his lifetime he wrote and adopted more than seventy resolutions. He would read them each week to himself, reminding his heart of what his head had promised. Edwards was a rare man and it was a different time. I do not think in the culture we live in that many would subscribe to the process he did to move towards holiness. So we need to start small. Perhaps overtime the rules will gain sub-points, but I have purposed to keep it simple so that I, as I am a simple guy, can in some measure practice them. They are designed to put me on a path to worship which leads to joy.

In order to become a joyful, blessed, happy and even prosperous minority, we will have to learn what it means to worship. These rules are an aid to that end. As we enter in, we need to look to Jesus, and continue to walk in step with the Spirit.

I believe there are four rules that we can practice to help us become a healthy minority. As you read them, would you read them in context of the heart of this book? I do believe if we are to recognize our minority status and then become a healthy minority, we should practice these rules.

One last thought. The rules are not means of grace. The bible, the sacraments, prayer and the spiritual disciplines are means of grace. The rules will help you see if you are availing yourself of the means of grace. They are not to be graded. They are pointers to point us to Him.

Minority Rules

#1 The Rule of Freedom
"You shall know the truth and the truth will set you free"
                                                            Jesus

If we are to be a healthy minority we must believe that we *are* a minority and we must believe, in practice that we are at the same time free. Hopefully I convinced you early on that we are a minority. That fact changes everything. But, just because we are a minority does not mean that we should have the attitude of those in bondage. The bible is a history book that details the setting free of our people. Some of us, some of the time, live as if we have returned to some place like Egypt. We live as captives, not remembering that we have been set free from the penalty for sin, the power of sin, the approval of man and any other idol god. Freedom was delivered to us in the person and work of Christ and it came with huge benefits.

We are friends of Jesus, God has adopted us and He has made us sons and daughters. We need to walk in that truth daily. There are many examples in scripture of people saying they were followers of Jesus, but not really following after Him because they were in bondage to something else. We are free to live for Him, knowing that we are secure. We are free to follow passionately after Christ by continually learning in all things, by working joyfully for His kingdom to come, and by stewarding our time and talents.

There is freedom in just *being* and, from that being, good should flow to others with no pressure to "do." We, as a people, are free and the majority cannot take that away from us. Education is a key to knowing true freedom. For centuries, God's people did not have access to the Word. Now we have no excuse. If we think the Word of God is living and active and powerful, if we really believe that, we will spend time in it and continually re-discover the beauty of the freedom we have in Christ. All of us need some help to do that. We call that help being a disciple and having someone who is further down the road teach you, encourage you and even correct you.

As truth washes over our heart, mind and soul it will create a hunger for communion and community. When we are enslaved by fear and worldly pursuits we should repent and ask for faith to believe. That is easier said than done because, even though we can ask for forgiveness, I often find that I will forget to, or avoid it. Our religion calls us to identify sin, repent and ask for faith. That is where the rule of community, as we shall discuss, is helpful.

In my personal story I need to say this may be my biggest struggle, to know that I am free. I can often find myself acting like God does not know me and He is not out for my good. I can get so wrapped up in what I think I need to control my life, that joy is sapped out of my life.

I live in bondage. The Apostle Paul told the Galatians they were foolish. He would have stronger words for me I am sure. I want to live in freedom, but my nature keeps telling me otherwise and I foolishly listen to the world around me that says I can never be free. That is very, very stupid.

Minority Rules

To make matters worse I often lean towards creating what mathematicians call a "bounded set" instead of a centered set. Other authors have described this better than I will here I am sure. Bounded sets occur when we set up fences around our community stating, "You cannot do this and you must do that!" The walls keep people out and create opportunities for sin in the lives of those who are inside of the community. Give someone a word picture and they will dwell on it.

Centered sets are focused on what is at the center. I am thinking that is perhaps what our community should be more like. Christ is the center. We should focus on Christ and the freedom He brings. I am not for lawlessness, but I think if we begin to focus on freedom in Christ, the law will become a tool to help us realize and breathe our freedom, not a curse that holds us in bondage. Further, as we fix our eyes on Christ, those outside of our community will see that we are not talking at them over a fence, insisting they must climb it to become one of us. They will see us looking at Him and they might look too.

To further complicate matters, sometimes I can trade the word free for independent. My natural man wants to be independent. That character trait is reserved for God alone and as I pursue it I become more devilish. Any smell of that in my life has to be sniffed out and should move me to a hatred of it and then to repentance.

So, how do we live as free men and women? I would suggest we talk it out a lot. Our friends in Alcoholics Anonymous have given us a clue. "Hi, my name is Randy and I am a recovering slave of sin." Unless we can walk the walk and talk the talk we will not make much progress here.

Humbly admitting we were powerless is a good place to start, continue and finish our lives. We need others around us who will admit the same. Secret Christianity is a sham. Let's go public with who we were and what we have become by the grace of God. Freedom is our battle cry, but it must be made with other voices, shouting as one, "We are free!" The rule of community is helpful to that end.

#2 The Rule of Community
"Everyone, everyone, will be a member of a gang. The only question is which gang."

Presbyterian Pastor

One reason we do not live as free men and women is because we have to look good. People really would not like us if they knew who we were. So we hide personally, professionally and spiritually. Adam gave us the idea in the garden.

Isolation breeds massive amounts of mistrust, selfishness and cynicism. The comedian George Carlin once said he knew a way to end all wars. Everyone line up in two lines and then go from person to person shaking hands and introducing yourself. When it was over, we would never be able to fire a shot across the line because we would say, "Hey wait a minute. I know that guy!" I wish that could be reality.

Minority Rules

I have added my own thinking to his. If we all had a good cry on one another's shoulder we would be a bit more empathetic and less callous. In order to do that, we need to get closer.

We are withdrawn; neighbor from neighbor, churchman from churchman and family member from family member. Who can create community? The church should. I am thinking that churches should re-adopt the old parish mindset; a geographical boundary in which they intend to serve all of the people who live there. Simply put we need to define who the parishioners are and then help one another economically, socially, educationally, and in any other way that would be good for the kingdom to come. That could include being in one another's lives; a scary thought for Americans.

I remember growing up on the south side of Milwaukee and living in a parish. It was the same parish that my grandparents, aunts, uncles and cousins in part lived in. The sense of community was deep and often scary for a young boy who had a propensity to be a young boy. People knew people.

The same word picture can be seen for the immigrants who came to America at the turn of the century. Italians helped Italians; Germans helped Germans and Poles the Poles. Those who had been there awhile helped new people to the community. Business contacts were made, loans provided, clothes given; people helping people who were like them. That is the heart of a healthy community, a community we should be like.

Minority Rules

They did it because they had a mission and a cause that was greater than them. They knew they needed to band together in order to not just survive but be prosperous in the world they lived in. Christians need to know that the idea for community was around a long time before my great grandfather got off the boat from Poland. It is a biblical pillar.

Following Jesus by your self is not the gospel. You are not a minority of one. You are part of a minority group and God is calling you and me and others to band together for the sake of His name and our health. Our religion is community based and we are not following if we are not following *with* others.

We serve the blessed triune God, a God who *is* community and His path to joy and power is the pathway that includes other people. As a minority group we need to be with one another, pray for one another, encourage one another and exhort one another.

There is very much to be learned through the rule of community. In community we find people who are further along than we are; people we can learn from. Sometimes they are called mentors or disciplers and sometimes they are called pastors or shepherds. All of us need someone in our life who is further along. The Bible is full of descriptive stories of people living out the gospel in community and being led by leaders. Community is not just an aid; it is an essential. If you will admit your minority status and then gather together with others who are like you, you will begin to see the power of the minority because once we enter into true community we can grow and we can celebrate.

So how do we move towards community? I think we may have to change the way we do church. Want to join the church? Then perhaps you really need to commit to be in a small group led by a leader who knows a bit of something. Maybe we should not have "independent" members. If you are a Christian, we want you to be part of the life we are doing together. Churches should be responsible to help network believers together for the common good. Education, jobs, support, exhortation and more should be some of the ties that bind us together. In today's fast paced society it may mean that members of the church will have to do one less "club" in the world, but the benefits should be worth the investment of time.

Community means something else too. It means that people are close enough to be examined. I know that is anathema to Americans. To have anyone look at anything we do, seems to be against the Constitution. As Christians, we will be healthier if we let others examine us. Most of us walk around nominally healthy or even unhealthy spiritually speaking and worse yet, we may not even know it because we have no baseline by which to measure.

If you were under the weather, any good physician would say, "Come on in and let's run a few tests." As an example, I did not know I had high cholesterol until the doctor ran the test. I thought I was fine, but the test proved otherwise. Even though the state of the soul cannot be measured as blood pressure can, God has given us the ability as a church to test and see how we are doing spiritually in order that we can encourage one another towards a healthier way of living out the gospel. So we need to think a bit about what it means to "check our spiritual pulse" and see if we are in need of a change in diet or maybe even a prescription.

Bottom line? Our religion is one of community. Our God is a god of community. He is three in one and He invites us in to the fellowship of the Father, Son and Holy Spirit. If we are not in community we may not be in the religion.

#3 The Rule of Celebration
"GOAL!"   *Spanish football fan*

We are born with a desire to celebrate. The world would say we should spend our "celebration tokens" on sports, business success, money, sexual conquests or other worldly goods. Jesus said in so many words, "You can't celebrate me and money!" When we do celebrate mammon, we lose our ability to celebrate what is even better: Jesus. It goes back to that brain attic example of our friend Sherlock Holmes. You cannot celebrate all things; your brain and soul cannot hold onto them all.

It is very strange to me that in general Christians are not known for celebrating well. I am not talking about happy clappy worship. Some of our brothers and sisters worship in exuberant styles that can be joyful and yet off-putting for some. They would say, "Who has a birthday party by themselves or celebrates a good day alone? Celebration

Minority Rules

is meant to take place in community! Personal study and meditation are helpful to the soul of a believer, but celebration is an activity for our community as a whole to enter into and we should have some joy about it!"

I make no judgment on raising hands, dancing and shouting for worship to be great. When I speak of celebration, though, I am saying we should be joyful and celebrate the abundant life, Monday through Sunday. Some of us are angry and cynical. Many of us would not be able to remember the last time we laughed until we cried. A few of us are secretly or openly prohibitionists of anything fun.

We are called to worship God and *enjoy* Him. Our rule should be to do so and we should do that often as a community. The heart of celebrating God is rejoicing in our corporate and individual identity in Christ and living lives together that bear out His image as imprinted in us. The Rule of Celebration shows us how to live together with an attitude of thanksgiving that we are a minority by His providence. If we are to be healthy, we must look to the One who is the giver of health and rejoice in Him.

Celebration can take on various forms. It can be as simple as singing or serving or sharing or it could be soliciting the King for what the community believes would be good for the kingdom. It can be feasting too.

How might we live a life of celebration? Certainly we could all take a look at what our weekend services might look and feel like. Beyond that, we need to celebrate

Jesus as we live in our communities, where we work and where we play. We should all aspire to be bosses like Fezziwig, sons like Tiny Tim and employees like Bob Cratchit. We should be joyful in who we are and celebrating who He is all the days of our life. Celebration is not a moment in time; it is our lives, even when times are hard. We rejoice even in sorrow. No other religion does that.

We need to rejoice in our Lord, no matter what the circumstances. Jesus is the Great Rejoicer. Even in times of tribulation and persecution we can know that we are the King's people and as such we are called for a joyful purpose. Nothing can separate us from His love so, why wouldn't we be joyful all the time. And why wouldn't we go about joyfully fulfilling the purpose He has for us? That purpose is surprising and counter intuitive. We are called to wash feet.

4 The Rule of Foot Washing
"I came not to be served, but to serve"   Jesus

My good friend Nittin Sardar will most likely have an epitaph of; "Foot Washer" on his tombstone. He is part of a minority in India who leads a church planting movement and he has understood the beauty of washing the feet of others. His ministry lovingly touches widows, farmers, street cleaners and others that society would view as untouchable.

His ministry does not have much to give, but they give what they have; they wash feet and they pray for people.

Minority Rules

We are called to have a high regard for the community of those who believe along with us by helping one another, serving one another and caring for one another deeply. The Rule of Foot Washing helps us ask ourselves if we have helped a brother or sister in Christ spiritually, financially, emotionally or otherwise. Have we helped the community's "tide" be lifted and along with it all the boats of believers? Have we truly forgiven one another and are we joyfully considering others better than ourselves? Do we give sacrificially and are we praying blessings upon one another? Questions, like that, will help us see if we are living the Rule of Foot Washing.

One caution here is that every natural thing inside of me wants to get my feet washed. You may want to have someone serve you too. The bottom line here is that there is more joy in giving than receiving and you cannot wash the feet of others while yours are being washed. Even Jesus did not do that. Look to Him. He is the one who on the evening of the great supper bent down and washed everyone's feet, Judas included. He was the one who said He did not come to be served, but to serve and give His life. He is the one who is even serving you now as you read this page. He is the one who will always serve you. Forever. No other religion has a God like that. He is the one who will enable you to wash feet as He helps you see that He did, does and will wash yours.

The Rule of Foot Washing does not end with our community. We are called to wash the feet of those God has created. That means many men and women. It also means we are to love them unreasonably by serving, giving and blessing all people with no hidden agenda of conversion. You will not do this with great success alone. You need others to go with you, to serve with you and to exhort you to wash feet in your community. Only Jesus can do it alone and even that was by the power of the Spirit.

So, do we need a bucket and soap? I do. Perhaps you could take them to your neighbor's house and offer to wash her windows. Maybe you are called to just listen on the phone to someone who is hurting or perhaps you need to give some money away. I am sure you can think of a hundred ways to serve. My guess is that you will fear getting exhausted as you begin to engage with the Rule of Foot Washing. You may. I encourage you to be rhythmic. Get and give, get and give and get and give.

You need to be filled with the Spirit to know you are free. You need to live in community to enter in to others' lives and you need to remember to celebrate Him well. You have nothing to give. He will give you what you need to give away to others. As you get a bit "less full," check yourself to make sure you know you are free, you are in a loving community and you are celebrating with joy.

Questions to ponder

1. Discuss the idea of knowing you are free in Christ. Can you put into your own words what that means? What hinders you from thinking you are free in Christ?

2. Are you in a community that helps you grow? What keeps community from become "plastic" or false? What is the role of the leader of the community?

3. What type of "celebration" personality do you have? How do you express joy? When is it hard to celebrate?

4. Have you ever had your feet washed or washed someone else's? Can you describe the experience? What would it mean, where you live, to "wash feet?"

Chapter Eight
The Power of Minority Rules

I began this book talking about power and that is a good place to end. Do you want power, the power of the resurrection in your life? The kind of power that makes dead things come to life, that heals and restores, and that changes hearts?

Then love.

To love you have to know that you are forgiven and free. You have to be in a healthy community and learn to celebrate. Then you can joyfully wash other people's feet. That will change the world and press our movement forward. You also need to know that you cannot do it in your own strength. Jesus is the foot washer and He is the one who will compel you to love with joy as you look to Him, as you are reminded of the cross and as you run to the resurrection. The power of the resurrection is found in our ability to love to the death, while washing the feet of our enemies.

If we will unlock again the secrets of the power of the minority rules, we will change the world. Jesus is freedom, He is community and He is to be celebrated as He leads us, the minority, to love even as He does.

What it could look like

So what could it look like? There is no point in keeping rules if you do not enjoy the keeping of them and if you do not see benefit from doing so. The kingdom is now and it is yet to come so we should in some measure both have joy as we experience it *and* at the same time wait patiently for the full benefits of it. That might even mean that we suffer for a little while. Having said that, if we practiced the minority rules I think our world could look a little more, and a little less, like this:

Inside our Community

1. More *re-creational* activities. I am not an avid golfer, boater, tennis player or swimmer, although I have done all of the above. I think it is great to have some recreation, but I would encourage us all to seek what may be even better. *Re-creation* can be found in serving the poor, working on a friend's house or doing a fun run for charity. Through re-creation we may just find our souls are rejuvenated. I am suggesting that some recreational time and resources could be used for other needs in the world. I am sure I will get an argument on that. You can include movies, TV and maybe some books in this category. How much do we need to be entertained? Granted, some forms of entertainment can be energizing and I am not proposing prohibition on sports and recreation but I am suggesting that it is over realized in our culture. From kids on baseball teams to video games to women in tennis leagues, it can, for many, take the place of time spent loving and serving others. As we live the rules, I think we will find that our leisure and

entertainment become intertwined with our service to those who have less than we do. Jesus said He came not to be served but to serve. That is significant. Other kings want to be served. Not Jesus. He said, "Do like I do." So, go out and serve. Guess what you may have to give up to do that? Leisure and entertainment. If we lived the rule, we would joyfully serve one another. This truth is so embedded in the gospel that in great measure it *is* the gospel. The closer we get to serving others, the closer we get to the heart of God.

2. More Education. We would be chief among learners. For the Christian, learning should be a lifelong exercise. The sad truth is that learning is hard work and you need to give up something to get it. For those of you who have enrolled in a graduate program while working a full time job, you know what I mean. If Christians lived out minority rules, we would see our need for more education, formal as well as informal. Specifically we might try to begin to really know and understand the bible. Our lack of ability to apologize is frightening and our lack of understanding about other worldviews is startling. As we live in community and celebrate and go out into the world to wash feet, we will run to education. Exercising leads to hunger. As we minister we will need the Word to both answer questions and replenish our souls. We call that discipleship. If you want to know more about that

talk with a man like Randy Pope through Life on Life Discipleship at Perimeter Church. He has developed, over 30 years, a way to educate men and women that is life changing.

3. More Compassion. We should love one another and others at a cost. The word compassion means to suffer with. When we recognize our status, we will be able to enter into other people's pain. We will do that by serving, by giving and even by suffering. We tend to turn off the TV when we see too much misery, or turn it on when we experience too much. We need to be active in serving and not worry about the pain. We need to give of our time and treasures. We have loads of stuff in our basements and attics that would benefit many. Keeping it makes us fat. We should give it away and be healthy. This area of compassion should include issues we have consistently avoided. It will include compassion for those who come after us by thinking about recycling, driving a car with good gas mileage and generally becoming more eco friendly. This may sound stupid, but I think ecology is such a basic "lets see how they really live issue" that if we are to have any platform in the 21st century with unbelievers, we will need to at least rise to the top 25% of the pack in this area.

4. More family. This is a hard topic to discuss. If we were healthier we would have more kids and be engaged in family. I do not think you could

convince me that a population explosion is in danger of overtaxing natural resources. So why do we not have more kids? We are allegedly pro life and yet we use birth control at a similar rate as others. Something is wrong with the picture. Our actions do not line up with our beliefs. Our community could be bigger by procreation and/or by adoption of some of the 140 million orphans in the world.

Outside our community

What about outside of our community? Should we expect to have any impact on the world? I think so but, as we are a minority, we need to remember that we will not solve all the problems of the world or even very many. We do want, and this is important, to know that wherever we go, the smell of the aroma of the gospel lingers after we leave. We have to preach the gospel in word and deed. There can be no compromise on that issue. Social work is worthless without the gospel of Christ at its heart.

We could as a group pick a few problems and focus our resources there. A few key things are important to remember here as my friend Nittin suggests. We need to understand the balance of power. They are bigger than we are so we are foolish to get on our high horse in the public square and shoot arrows at the bull. We also need to understand contextualization. If we are in Rome, we need to put some Roman clothes on. Remember they are not like us, but we are called to reach out to them. What would that look like? Here are just a few word picture

Minority Rules

ideas. They may not be *the* ideas but they will prevent us from becoming isolationists.

1. More clean and living water. Bono has a point that is hard to fully execute on. Maybe because he has bitten off "Africa." I would not suggest that. I would suggest we as a minority choose other smaller but identifiable minorities, who are far worse off than we are and help them get good water to drink so they can live. We should pick a small group and do it well, sharing with them resources we have and the knowledge we have about living water. Then another and then another. This will not happen until Christians collectively realize we are a minority, band together and figure out that part of our road to healthiness is found in helping others. Yes, the poor will always be with us, but I am not sure there should be as many as there are and I think we should get them clean water. We are the only agency that can give them clean water *and* living water at the same time. They need both.

2. More justice and less sex trade. Jesus had a high regard for women and He told us men to look out after them. He commands us to justice. He also had a word or two to say about the widows and orphans and how we should love them. We can stand in the gap for those who are being raped around the world. They are a minority. Again, if we try to tackle the issue in the macro, we will fail. The church militant should pick a spot and pour in

resources. The underpinnings of the sex slave trade are many and varied from economic issues to legal to social. A lot of work has to go in here to make a true difference.

I could have said more live births (less aborted), more housing, less poverty or countless other social ills. Perhaps others think those are more important. They may well be. What is more important than all of them is that we love people with the truth of the gospel.

Thanks for reading this far. I am thinking, praying and wondering what I need to do differently with my life if I am to live out what I believe to be true. I want to encourage you to think, to study, and to test for yourself what I have said here. I would love to get feedback. I am sure, that I wrote something that is not true, inadvertently offended a people group, or said something that does not make sense at all. If I have in any way, let me know. I would welcome discussion. I have a lot more questions myself. I do believe that we are called to live as a minority here on earth; a healthy minority. As we grasp and own that concept we will live in a beautiful way for God and the kingdom will come in a richer way.

I hope and pray we will not float like dead men and that we will not be a bitter, "against the world" minority. I pray that we will exude the confidence of a people who have been redeemed, a people who have freedom and assurance of their destiny and can rest in the work of Christ, loving His creation, as they await His return.

Questions to ponder

1. What are your thoughts on leisure and recreational activities?

2. Describe the last really formal education you participated in. Have you ever taken a continuing education class and if so how was it helpful? Do you think discipleship programs are useful to education of Christians and how can they balance classroom with the real world?

3. What level of concern do you have for clean water and justice? Do you think the Christian community should narrow its focus on a few areas and people or is it better to be broadly based and helping many?

4. What other questions do you have, or comments, after reading this book?

Onward Afterward

A few questions come to mind as I complete this work. Will we get smaller? If we are a minority, how small will we get? I don't know, but I do imagine we will get smaller, the trend seems to be heading in that direction and the growth rate of other religions (and "no religion") is far outpacing us, so I presume we will get smaller for a generation or two. After that who knows? This much I do know, When I look in the annals of history of our people, God tends to expand the influence and size of the community living on earth when it "turns from its ways and turns back to Him" so perhaps we will have the distinct privilege of setting the stage for the next generation.

I am wondering how I will live now that I have written this. Maybe a good word to describe my life going forward will be "try." I will try to thank God daily for making me a minority. I will try to have a higher regard for those in our community, I will try and worship by following after Jesus and I will try to love people outside of our community by serving and giving while proclaiming truth.

I believe I will be happier as I try and in the trying I will be happier too. I do not expect to be very successful, but here is my hope: if others will do the same; give thanks, have a higher regard, worship by following and discharge the debt to love, somehow I believe we will together make an impact and have greater joy as a community. I am living now to that end. So my last question is, "Who is with me (or who am I with)?"

Minority Rules

I love "Les Miserables". It is simply the best musical ever. It is about grace and the law, sin and salvation, forgiveness and bitterness, sacrifice and greed. In the closing song the whole ensemble concludes with, "Do you hear the people sing?" One of the verses says, "Who will be strong and stand with me? Somewhere beyond the barricade is there a world you long to see?"

That may be our question to ask one another because I am sure it is being asked of us as Christians. Who will be strong and stand with Me? The barricade is multifaceted. It is my sin: my selfish desire to have personal peace and affluence, it is the culture I live in that says, "Have fun," it is even found in the schemes of the evil one and it is the institutionalization of the church.

I think it was Fidel Castro who once said, "Yesterday's revolutionaries are today's bureaucrats" Great quote. Whatever you think of Castro, he remained true to his ideals at great expense. He led a small nation in the shadow of a superpower; a minority cause if there ever was one.

That is a great word picture for the church. We are revolutionaries at heart. Let's press forward knowing freedom has been bought, living in communion, celebrating the victory and giving ourselves away for the cause of the king as we await His return. He will come, the revolution will be over, and then we will be able to rejoice in a fuller way as we recount the stories of how we lived out the minority rules.

An Apologetic

This may seem like an odd place to put the most important thing. I told you at the beginning that I liked authors who spelled out what their worldview is. I hope I have done that in this book. I am guessing that most who read this book are Christians. For those of you who profess to be followers of Jesus I will remind you and me that the gospel is the power of God for salvation of everyone who believes. So I encourage you to read on. For those wondering about Christianity here it is in a nutshell:

The Bible: is about what God has done, is doing and will do to reconcile relationships.

The Old Testament: Tells the story of God creating, man deciding to be his own god and God lovingly restoring the ensuing broken relationship in the short term by calling a people (the Israelites) to himself. It is a picture of what is to come.

The New Testament: Jesus, who is God, was born of a virgin, and lived a perfect life. He never sinned. He went to death on a cross to pay for our sin, rose and conquered the grave. That is it. Jesus (no one seriously disputes he was a historical figure) died around AD 33. No one really disputes that either. Then (here is the disputed part) he rose from the grave. The whole time he was alive (before he died and rose again) he said he would do it and he claimed to be God. He also said stuff like "I forgive you of your sins."

Minority Rules

Only God should do that.
Only God can do that.
Only God does do that.

Jesus is God and He in part proved that by raising himself from the dead.

So the choice is pretty simple. Believe or do not believe it. The "it" is Him. I have found believing it is a good thing, because I had more unanswered questions when I did not believe it. Questions like, "What about suffering?" and "Why was I created?" and "How can I have some joy?" were answered in fuller measure when I began to believe. Not that all my problems are solved. That is in part why I wrote this book. But, I can say I now see my problems in a better light. I know that good things are happening in my life because of what God is doing, not because of what I am doing. That takes some pressure off. That helps my anxious thoughts. I am no longer Don Quixote. I am just an adopted son and grateful to be so.

One other cool thing I have discovered. My prayers are always answered. Sound unbelievable? It is true. The answer is always yes or better. Janis Joplin once wrote a song, "O Lord won't you buy me a Mercedes Benz, my friends all drive Porsches I must make amends. Worked hard all my lifetime no help from my friends, so oh Lord won't you buy me a Mercedes Benz?" Those are creative prayer lyrics, but not prone to be answered in the affirmative. Questions about prayer abound. What should I pray for? Why are my prayers not answered? How come I never have a desire to pray?

Minority Rules

Some people ask, "If God knows everything and will accomplish what He wants, why should we pray?" Good question. Have you ever thought that part of His plan *requires* prayer? It is not the initial cause of His actions, but because of His character, He has to respond. He does not have a "Nobody Home" sign on the door. He will answer one of two ways to the person who calls on Him in faith: Yes or Better. Those are the two options.

Paul tells the Romans that God "works all things together for good to those who love God." If that is you, your prayers will be yes or better. Our challenge is seeing that if the answer is not yes, it is better. Jesus says, he is not going to give us a stone if we ask for bread. He will do right by us; by His perfect knowledge of what is best for us, He will direct and that is good. His character dictates that He loves His people and that He does right by them for His glory.

C.S. Lewis once said that he was glad God had not answered yes to many of his prayers. God had "better" in mind and over time Lewis could look back and see that was indeed the case.

Lastly, I would put this in smaller font if I could; I am a "Calvin kind of guy." Just to clear that up, here is what I mean. I believe that God is sovereign. He rules over all of His creation and He governs their actions. God is triune (three in one) and God is before time began, as we know it. He made a covenant with Himself to create and redeem a people for His glory. God the Father created,

Minority Rules

Jesus the Son redeemed, and the Holy Spirit applies the work of redemption to those God loves with a sovereign distinguishing love. So, God does all the work. Once he "makes me alive" I respond to Him, by the faith that He has given me. So I am at His mercy and that is a good thing.

Having said that, He has given us free will, under the umbrella of His sovereignty and we are called to use the gifts we have been given for the sake of His name. That means we are called to be a blessing and stand up against the things that are not of the blessed triune God we serve. I find that very easy to say and very hard to do.

So I am perhaps behind you. I don't know. But I do know I always set time aside for people who want to discuss and learn. I welcome an opportunity to talk with you via email, phone or even in person. I usually provide coffee or tea.

Blessings

RS

Questions to ponder

1. What are your thoughts on the "apologetic appendix?"

2. Have your prayers been answered? Have you ever thought that the answer was "better?" If you adopt that view, how might that change the way you pray and the frequency with which you pray?

3. Everyone has some theological grid. If you can, take some time and explain yours.

Minority Rules

Minority Rules

To Katherine, Adam, Lyla, Logan, Allison, Dan and Sarah

I love you! And you are next. Sorry my generation was a patchwork quilt of holding to our values and forgetting them. Your generation will be the next standard bearers of our minority group. Would you please remember one thing: God always uses the smallest, the youngest, and the weakest. He *always* uses His minority group to accomplish the great things He has decreed. Always. Size is not necessarily an indicator of success. He will use you as look to Him and as He lavishes His great love upon you during this life.

CPSIA information can be obtained
at www.ICGtesting.com
Printed in the USA
LVHW091454060220
646074LV00001BA/276